Discovering Cadborosaurus

The carcass of a probable juvenile Cadborosaurus found in the stomach of a whale in 1937. See pages 85 to 95. (Photo: Public domain)

Discovering Cadborosaurus

Paul LeBlond PhD
John Kirk III
Jason Walton

Edited by:

Christopher L. Murphy

hancock

house

ISBN 978-0-88839-735-5 [print]
ISBN 978-0-88839-735-6 [e-book]

Library and Archives Canada Catalogue in Publication

LeBlond, Paul H., PhD (Paul Henri)
Kirk, John A. (John Anthony)
Walton, Jason N. (Jason Nicholas)
Discovering Caborosaurus

Includes bibliographical references and index.
ISBN 978-0-88839-735-5

Editor: Christopher L. Murphy
Book design: Christopher L. Murphy
Front Cover artwork and design: Jason Walton

Printed in the USA

We acknowledge the financial support of the Government of Canada through the Canada Book Fund for our publishing activities.

Published simultaneously in Canada and the United States by:

HANCOCK HOUSE PUBLISHERS LTD.
19313 Zero Avenue, Surrey, B.C. Canada V3Z 9R9
(604) 538-1114 Fax (604) 538-2262
HANCOCK HOUSE PUBLISHERS
#104-4550 Birch Bay Lynden Rd, Blaine, WA U.S.A.
98230-9436 (800) 938-1114 Fax (800) 983-2262
Website: www.hancockhouse.com
Email: sales@hancockhouse.com

Contents

Note on Measurements: This book uses the Imperial/USA measurement units. The metric conversions are as follows:

1 Inch = 2.54 centimeters
1 Foot = 30.48 centimeters
1 Yard = 0.91 meter
1 Mile = 1.61 kilometers
1 Pound = 0.45 kilogram

Acknowledgements

This is a book about discovery, and our deepest appreciation goes to all those courageous people who have braved ridicule to describe the unusual animals that they have seen. They are the discoverers and without them we would not know about Cadborosaurus. We are also grateful to all our friends and collaborators who have encouraged us in this rather eccentric pursuit over the years. Special thanks to John Sibert, who was there right at the beginning, to the late Jim Clark, co-founder of the British Columbia Scientific Cryptozoology Club, and to Ed Bousfield, for his scientific guidance and enthusiasm through an earlier version of this account and his permission to use some previously published material. Frank Holm discovered many accounts of early Caddy encounters in local historical publications. Chris Murphy read the manuscript with the critical eye of an experienced cryptozoological communicator and made valuable suggestions for improvement. Any errors or misinterpretations are of course our responsibility and we invite feedback from our readers through the CaddyScan website.

Introduction

Cadborosaurus, or more familiarly Caddy, is the name given to a large marine animal sighted by hundreds of eye-witnesses in the coastal waters of the northeast Pacific Ocean. While reliable observers affirm that Caddy is an unknown creature, no specimen has ever been available for scientific examination; nearly all the evidence for its presence remains anecdotal. Descriptions provided by witnesses are still insufficient to pronounce on its zoological nature. Furthermore, there are strong indications that more than a single type of animal might hide under the name. Caddy thus remains a "cryptid," an undiscovered creature, whose existence and nature remain unrecognized by mainstream science.

This book is a contribution to Caddy's discovery, a collective process which is still on-going and has to date been generally uncoordinated. By introducing the reader to the available evidence and its analysis, as well as providing a web portal for reporting encounters, we hope to improve the quality and reliability of future sighting reports, strengthening the evidence for Caddy's existence by familiarizing future witnesses with Caddy's distinguishing features and avoiding mistaken descriptions.

Discovery and classification of the world's living fauna has long been a fundamental preoccupation of zoologists. Although much progress has been made since Linnaeus applied his system of binomial nomenclature to animals in 1758, a complete inventory is still beyond reach. A recent study by Mora et al.[1] claims that only 10% of the world's species of living organisms have been discovered. Extrapolation predicts a total of 8.74 million eukaryote[2] species on Earth; of these over 7 million would be animals, of which less than a million have so far been discovered and catalogued.

The discovery of a new animal usually involves the intentional or accidental capture of a specimen, followed by a careful examination of its features and, lately, of its genetic make-up through DNA

---

1. Mora et al., 2011
2. Eukaryote species have nucleated cells. All multicellular organisms: animals, plants and fungi, are eukaryotes.

analysis. Scientific publication of a description of a type specimen, preferably accessible to further scrutiny, normally leads to acceptance and incorporation of the new species within the recognized fauna. The International Code on Zoological Nomenclature sets the rules for the naming of animals and for resolving nomenclatural problems.[3]

Discovery is however not always a cut and dry capture-and-classify process. The existence of an animal is sometimes known, especially to people sharing its environment, well before some zoologist happens to come along to capture it. Such knowledge, especially of rare and elusive animals, may precede capture of a specimen by a long time. During such a limbo period, the animal obviously exists, in spite of its lack of official scientific description, which after all bestows only recognition, not existence. Such animals are called cryptids.[4] Naturalists interested in elucidating the mystery surrounding their existence are called cryptozoologists, a term introduced in the 1960s by French zoologist Bernard Heuvelmans who wrote extensively about unknown animals.

Cryptozoology, as defined by Heuvelmans,[5] is the science of hidden, meaning "undescribed by science" animals. Its basic objective is to accumulate all available information on still hidden species to assist in an eventual positive zoological recognition. At some point, to quote paleontologist Yves Coppens,[6] there is enough information that " creatures pass from the realm of cryptozoology

---

3. iczn.org/code

4. Best known cryptids include the yeti, the sasquatch, and Nessie: the Loch Ness "monster." The term "cryptid" was coined by John Wall, as a more appropriate term than "monster," for animals whose existence remained unproven. International Society of Cryptozoology Newsletter, 2, (20), 1983.

5. Heuvelmans, 1982

6. Yves Coppens, eminent French paleontologist, co-discoverer of Lucy, the female *Australopithecus afarensis:* "It [cryptozoology] is a perfectly respectable science...It coexists very well with zoology. Each year, a number of creatures pass from the realm of cryptozoology to that of zoology... All there is to it is that once fully documented, they go from one list to another." www.rhedae-magazine.com/, Sat. Oct 20, 2007.

to that of zoology" ...or are dismissed a mere fables. The epistemological framework of the particularly lengthy discovery process of a very controversial cryptid, the Sasquatch, has been brilliantly analyzed by John Bindernagel.[7]

That there might remain undiscovered species in the ocean is widely expected.

The recently completed Census of Marine Life project, a 10-year international collaboration aiming at a better understanding of marine biodiversity, discovered thousands of new species.[8] Mora et al. estimated that 91% of ocean dwellers have yet to be discovered: millions of new species! However, most of these are likely to be microscopic organisms: most of the marine biomass—algae, bacteria, viruses—is too small to see with the naked eye: "the oceans are a microbial world, not a pond of fishes, dolphins and whales." [9]

Nevertheless, although there might be very few large animals left to discover in the oceans, the prospect of finding new ones is of great interest to scientists as well as to the general public. Caddy, known from sightings by hundreds of mariners and shore dwellers, appears to be such a new species. While it has already received a scientific description[10] and although there is little doubt as to its existence, little is known about its nature and habits. What kind of creature is it? Is there only one kind? These questions pose serious zoological challenges and attract the keen interest of cryptozoologists.

This book documents the progress of the discovery of Cadborosaurus; it reviews the evidence for its existence, starting with archaeological and ethnographic sources and continuing with a selection of the most revealing and reliable eyewitness reports, presented in their own words. As most of what we know about Caddy stems from anecdotal observations, we have taken care to ensure that all reports satisfy two criteria: first, there must be no doubt, in the opinion of the witnesses as well as in ours, that what they saw was truly an animal, not a log, or waves or other inanimate object. Second, and even more critical, it must be clear that the animal seen

---

7. Bindernagel, 2010
8. Snelgrove, 2010
9. Pomeroy et al., 2007
10. Bousfield and LeBlond, 1995.

was truly of an unknown nature and not a seal, or whale or other familiar animal. We refer to the object of all such sightings as Caddy, although more than one kind of cryptid might hide behind that name.

The information gathered here comes from a variety of sources: published articles in local newspapers and magazines; a survey conducted in 1969 and published in 1973 by LeBlond and Sibert;[11] a scrapbook compiled by *Victoria Times* editor Archie Wills; and reports forwarded by eye-witnesses over the years to the present authors and to E. L. Bousfield. Many of these have been included in an earlier publication by LeBlond and Bousfield,[12] others have taken place or been discovered since then. Sightings listed in Appendix 1 include a reference to their original source, when known.

Based on such observations, on the analysis of the Naden Harbor carcass,[13] and on the opinions of some zoologists, we draw tentative conclusions about Caddy's nature and suggest further avenues of research. We invite the reader to experience the surprise, excitement and confusion arising from the gradual and continuing discovery of this elusive ocean denizen, a process in which they may well take part as future potential eye-witnesses. We also hope to attract the interest of imaginative scientists who, although well aware of the professional perils of cryptozoological research,[14] may be adventurous enough to bring their skill to the advancement of the discovery process.

---

11. LeBlond and Sibert, 1973
12. LeBlond and Bousfield, 1995
13. Found in 1937 in the stomach of a sperm whale and thought to be a juvenile Caddy (see Chapter 8, below).
14. On which, see Laurence, W. 2011, "The call of the weird: in praise of cryptobiologists." New Scientist, 22 June 2011. http://www.newscientist.com/article/mg21028176.000-the-call-of-the-weird-in-praise-of-cryptobiologists.html#.UrDl6mRDtst

Chapter 1
Caddy in Native Lore

Native Americans of the Pacific Northwest coastal areas, from California to Alaska, drew their livelihood from the sea and were intimately familiar with the local marine fauna. They collected shellfish, fished, and hunted sea mammals, including whales. Their oral tradition also abounds with stories of serpentine marine creatures which are clearly neither fish nor seals. While these animals are often mythified in a way which obscures their zoological nature, they are a precious source of cryptozoological information. In the words of Bernard Heuvelmans:

Mythology by Giorgio De Chirico (1934). (Photo: Public domain)

When one of these animals is eventually discovered by zoology and scientifically described, it is sometimes found that it was previously taken for an imaginary creature. Nevertheless, the beast in question, fated to be stripped some day of all its fancy attributes, has become, almost overnight, a well-authenticated new species, rising from a sometimes ludicrous folkloric reputation, and even a disputed cryptozoological fame, to a respectable zoological status.[1]

Mythification is of course not only to be found in pre-scientific societies. A striking modern example is offered by the subject

---

1. Heuvelmans, 1990

selected by the metaphysical artist Giorgio De Chirico to represent "Mythology." We shall encounter numerous variants of such a long-necked creature in the descriptions of Caddy by eye-witnesses.

The earliest clues about the existence of Caddy-like creatures are thus to be sought in the sea-serpent stories of coastal First Nations. For example, the Manhousat, from the west coast of Vancouver Island, British Columbia, spoke of an animal which they called hiyitl' iik: "he who moves by wriggling from side to side." In the words of Manhousat elder Luke Swan, "Sea-serpents were said to be seven or eight feet long. They moved very quickly, both on land and on water. They had legs, but when traveling on land, used their bodies more than their legs for propulsion,—moving like snakes."[2]

More surprisingly, sea serpents could grow wings at will! "Their head and back was covered with long hair, as is represented with strips of dyed red cedar bark on the sea-serpent mask." Sea serpents were rarely seen, especially in recent times. Mr. Swan's father had encountered one and shot an arrow at it but missed.

The cleverest cryptozoologist would have trouble imagining the animal hiding behind this story. Not an unusual situation. Take for example the iconic scene of the Lady and the Unicorn, pictured in the famous medieval draperies in Paris' Musée de Cluny. The animal depicted is clearly a goat with a horn on its head. The only resemblance between it and a rhinoceros or a narwhal, usually thought to be the source of the unicorn myth, is the horn, clearly an attachment providing little information about its original owner.

The sea-serpent HIYITL' IIK (Ellis and Swan, 1981). (Photo Theytus Books/P. Seesequasis used with permission.)

---

2. Ellis and Swan, 1981

A clearly more mythological creature was Sisiutl, the two-headed sea serpent of the Kwakiutl people of northern Vancouver Island. It could change shapes, and transform from animal to man and back at any time. Its effigy was used to ward off evil spirits.

Other coastal tribes also have stories about sea serpents. The Comox band, on the east side of Vancouver Island, spoke of the sea serpent Numkse lee Kwala; Comox elder Mary Clifton relates that on the way to Cape Mudge, at the north end of the Strait of Georgia, her relatives had seen a very long sea-serpent. "It

The Lady and the Unicorn. Musée de Cluny, Paris. (Photo: Public domain)

rose out of the water and then fell back with a loud crash. It was playful and did not hurt any of the number of people who saw it."[3] Henry Assu, of Cape Mudge wrote that a gigantic skate-like creature was commonly sighted near Maud Island in ancient times.[4] On the mainland side of the Strait of Georgia, the Sechelt mythology spoke of a friendly creature called T' chain-ko.[5] In contrast, the natives of Burrard Inlet (Vancouver harbour) spoke of Sayn Uskih ("Awful Snake"), a fearsome sea-serpent which, according to Captain Cates, former mayor of North Vancouver, " before the white man came, [it] lived a good deal of the time with its head resting on a rock just off Brockton Point, and its tail rippling out in the tidal stream." Even the fierce Haida from the north would not dare come through the narrows into Burrard Inlet because of its presence.[6] Further north, near Prince Rupert, an animal such as that described

3. Reimer, W. 1993
4. Taylor, J. 1999
5. White, H. 1994
6. Commercial Drive Monthly, Vancouver, Vol. 4, Issue 30, April 2000

by the Sampsons in 1934 was known to "the old people" as Zaweaksh, the monster of the sea, which they said they had known in the days of their youth."[7]

Artifacts preserve shape and forms which mere words often cannot convey faithfully. At numerous sites along the coast of British Columbia, local artists or shamans incised shallow engravings (known as petroglyphs) into prominent rock outcrops. The meaning of many of these icons has been lost. Human faces, salmon, sun symbols, sailing ships and other symbols can be recognized. There are also creatures that closely resemble the hiyitl' iik of Manhousat lore.

A striking example is the animal sketched at the Monsell site (shores of the Nanaimo River) which has an elongated body, four small legs (or flippers?) prominent teeth, a large eye and a mane (or horns?) on its head. A very similar creature, although missing back legs, is depicted in the Gabriola Island petroglyph site. Another such carving is found on a vertical face of a cliff at the water's edge on Sproat Lake,

Petroglyph from the Monsell si Nanaimo River, BC. (Hill and H 1974). (Photo: Public domain)

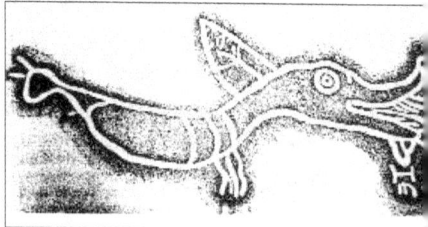

Petroglyph from Gabriola Island, B (Bentley and Bentley, 1981). (Pho Public domain)

Sproat Lake, Vancouver Island, Petroglyph. (Photo: Public domain)

Vancouver Island. While these petroglyphs are difficult to date, they are widely believed to predate the arrival of European explorers.

Another well-documented pre-contact artifact is the Skagit

---

7. Prince Rupert *This Week*, 15 Sept. 1996

River atlatl (spear-thrower), part of the collections of the world-famous Anthropology Museum of the University of British Columbia. This object has been carbon-dated to 1,700 (+/- 100) years before the present.[8] The atlatl is carved out of a piece of western yew (*Taxus brevifolia*). The handle is carved in the shape of a human head surmounted by that of a sea-monster reminiscent of those seen in petroglyphs, including some structure (mane? horns?) on top of its head, a large eye and large square teeth.

Drawing of the handle of the Skagit River atlatl (spear-thrower). (Photo: Authors' file)

Is hiyitl'iik, as depicted in Manhousat legends and in ancient artifacts, a representation of a real, live, still hidden animal, as cryptozoologists might believe, or a mythical creature like the thunderbird and the sisiutl?[9] Whether real or mythical, there clearly existed in local folklore, well before the arrival of European explorers and settlers, a solid tradition of a large serpentine marine animal: the earliest evidence for Cadborosaurus.

---

8. Fladmark et al., 1987
9. A two-headed sea serpent or snake with a human-like head in the middle of the body.

Chapter 2

Surprising Encounters

It didn't take very long for European explorers and fur traders arriving in the Pacific Northwest area in the late 18th century to encounter hiyitl'iik and its congeners. In the fall of 1791, while George Vancouver was still sailing across the Pacific towards the island that now bears his name, Robert Gray, an American fur-trader was in Clayoquot Sound, on the west coast of Vancouver Island, gathering sea otter pelts for the China market. One of his crew, John Hoskins, left an account of the voyage of the Columbia from Boston to the north-east Pacific.[1] On Oct 16, 1791, while hunting onshore in Tofino Inlet,..." ...one of the people who was with me," Hoskins wrote," saw a huge animal, very long with a large mouth and teeth, the neck about as thick as his thigh, tapered to the tail, with a black back and a light yellow belly..." Hoskins at first thought the animal was an alligator, but the natives told him that they knew of such an animal, with a head "something like a hound" and " the rest of the body in every way like a serpent." They called it Hieclick; it was a reptile, very scarce and "lived principally in the woods." The general description is reminiscent of Caddy as seen in native artifacts; it is also suggestive of the giant salamanders reported from Nitinat Lake (Chapter 7). The name Hieclick is most likely a variant spelling of hiyitl' iik, but that it "lived principally in the woods" is a bit of a stumbling block. Hoskins dismissed the animal as "magic;" in a footnote, the editor (Judge Howay) suggests that, "The animal was created by vivid Indian imagination." Cryptozoologists, on the other hand, used to partial and sometimes inconsistent descriptions, know how to withhold judgment without rejecting the information.

We have to wait nearly a century for further documented reports. In 1863, T.W. Graham, who was then building a saw-mill on Burrard Inlet, now Vancouver's harbour, reported seeing off Point Grey a "strange phenomenon, having the appearance of a female

---

1. Howay, F.C. 1990

with long hair of yellowish brown tinge drooping over the shoulders, the skin being dark olive... It gradually rose above the surface of the water within about thirty yards of where he was, showing the entire bust, in which position it remained for the space of five minutes... when it slowly sank into its native element." Two Indians who accompanied him were quite alarmed at the sight, seeing it as a dire omen.[2]

A few years later, in 1881, Frank Stannard, a pioneer Nanaimo merchant, but then just a boy of 12, was one of a party of six young people who were paddling a canoe off William Head (near Race Rocks, Juan de Fuca Strait) when suddenly there rose beside them a monster of "unknown habits." Plucky young Stannard pulled out his slingshot and let fly at one of the creature's "folds." The shot ricocheted off the serpent which then dived below the surface.[3]

Soon afterwards, in October 1888, Captain Edgar Avery of the barque Estrella reported sighting a large sea-serpent off the Umpqua River, Oregon. He described it as 80 feet long, big around as a barrel, holding its head 10 feet above the sea surface. Its head was flat and "about ten feet of what might properly be called the neck was covered with coarse hair, resembling a mane." [4]

While the above reports are rather sketchy, the encounter off the Queen Charlotte Islands in June 1897 related by prospector Osmond Fergusson provides much more detail. The description is contained in a letter found in the British Columbia Provincial Archives by archivist David Mattison[5]. In Fergusson's words (the square brackets are Mattison's):

About 4.30 this morning we left Caedoo [Kaidju?].[6] I was steering the boat and pushing an oar at the same time. There

2. British Columbian, New Westminster, 27 June 1863
3. Vancouver Province, 24, Aug. 1940, p. 5
4. New York Times, 28 Oct 1888
5. Mattison, D. 1964.
6. There are no villages by the name of Caedoo and three by the name of Kaidju (or Qai' dju) mentioned in Dalzell (1981). Of the three, the one located at the extreme southeast side of Moresby Island, near Benjamin Point facing Hecate Strait, is the most likely to have calm seas and be a safe port of call for two men in a small boat.

was no wind. The boat was 100 yards from shore, going south, with a fair tide. I saw ahead of us what I thought was a piece of driftwood. On getting closer, I noticed it was moving towards us. When within 50 yards, I said to Walker (my partner), What is that? It seems to be moving this way (against the tide). What we could see was an object like sketch (A) sticking out of the water about two feet. When within a few feet of it the end uncoiled and raised a long neck about five feet out of the water with a head like a snake [']s on it. The arched portion making a broad flat chest like I have seen on the cob[r]a I think.

When the serpent or whatever it was saw us it turned slightly towards land to avoid the boat. The head and neck were almost immediat[e]ly put under water again. As it passed the boat, at a distance, that with an effort, I could have thrown a[n] oar on it we could see a body about 25 feet long tapering with a fish like tail and I think a continuous fin running the length of the body.

A slow undulating motion went along the body, while the tail part had a steady sweep from side to side of about six feet. A curious thing was the broad neck or chest part that formed the arch (or hurricane dick, Walker called it). The only part out of water when the head was down was not exposed broadways in the direction the fish was going, but had a decided twist to the left allowing the water to flow through it.

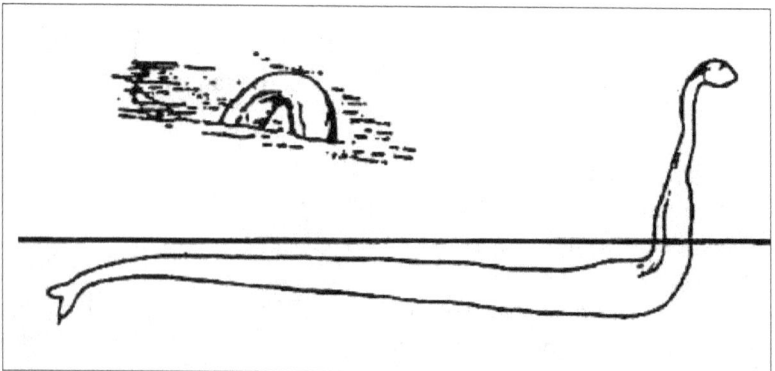

The animal seen by Fergusson and Walker off the Queen Charlotte Islands in 1897. (From Mattison, 1964). (Photo: Public domain)

Fergusson's description contains many elements common to such encounters: the witnesses' initial confusion about the nature of the object ("I thought it was a piece of driftwood"); their surprise at not recognizing it as a familiar animal; and their description of its unfamiliar features in terms of their resemblance to those of known animals.

A sea serpent was also seen near Victoria in the late 1800s. John "Long Gun" Irvine was deer hunting near Cormorant Point when he saw an animal in the ocean that at first, he thought was a horse, "but when I saw the length of it I knew it was something else and not a horse. I should judge it was all of twenty feet long and the only thing about it as I remember to make it look like a horse was its head. I started to shoot at it with my rifle, and I sure put some lead in that old sea serpent... the only effect of the shooting was to make it travel faster if that was possible." He wrote in his reminiscences, completed in 1942, of an event which he says happened "away back fifty years." As many other surprised and puzzled witnesses, he was "sure afraid to tell about it for I knew I would be laughed at and I would never hear the end of it."[7]

Another spectacular sighting by an experienced mariner, which left no doubt as to the unfamiliar nature of the animal seen, took place in March 1926 in Wright Sound, near the entrance to Douglas Channel (which leads inland to the town of Kitimat, BC). Captain C.J. House, a man with 31 years on deep sea and coastal vessels, was at the helm of the government fisheries patrol vessel *Cloyah*. House was not the sort of a man who would spin a yarn that would make him out as a fool; he was indeed rather reluctant to tell anyone about it.

The *Cloyah* had just entered Wright Sound, heading north, when the water roiled as if a whale swam just beneath the surface. As she came opposite Turtle Point, a head 18 inches wide and over two feet long rose from the commotion in the water. The neck followed, came up 'coiled up like a corkscrew' then straightened out when the head was some

---

7. Early Victoria. Reminiscences of Jack "Long Gun" Irvine, completed in September 1942, unpublished. BC Archives, Box MS0322.

30 ft above the water. For a half minute, the head was like a telephone pole. The sun, breaking through the clouds, cast a greenish gold tint to the creature's skin. Then, before the captain's eyes, the neck spiraled back down into the water. The body vanished, but for a long time the surface of the water churned as the creature's wake trailed away to sea." [8]

The animal seen by Captain House from the fisheries vessel *Cloyah*. (Photo: Debbie Mierau Graphic, used with permission.)

Later, in October of the same year, a similar long-necked creature was seen devouring salmon at the mouth of a stream near the head of Tahsis Inlet, on the west side of Vancouver Island.[9]

Many of these early encounters only came to light years after the event. Witnesses were often fearful of the ridicule which accompanies observations of unusual phenomena. Widely publicized sightings, such as those of October 1933, described below, or enquiries by investigating cryptozoologists, brought many old-time witnesses out of the closet. In response to a widely distributed expression of interest in sea serpents put out by LeBlond and Sibert

8. As told by Bruce Wishart in " Prince Rupert THIS WEEK," 15 Sep.1996
9. As told by Fred Olsen in The Daily Colonist, Victoria, Sunday April 16, 1967

in 1969, Philip H. Welch, then living in Port Alberni, BC, sent in the following account.

It was 1905, or perhaps 1906, Welch wasn't sure which year. He was then working for logging contractor Herb Tomlinson on Cracroft Island (on the east side of Johnstone Strait, off northern Vancouver Island), barking logs for horse-team hauling. On a September Sunday morning, he and a workmate borrowed the boss' 16-foot rowboat to go trout fishing across Johnstone Strait at the mouth of the Adams River. When they got there they discovered that there was an enormous run of pink salmon and that the river was so congested with salmon as to make it impossible to fish for trout. Although it was only about 9:00 a.m., the frustrated fishermen were resigned to having rowed in vain across the strait when, less than a mile from the mouth of the river, there appeared a long neck, emerging six to eight feet above the sea surface, about 200 yards from their boat. Welch wanted to shoot at it with his hunting rifle, but his companion talked him out of it, for fear that the creature might attack them. While they were arguing, the creature submerged, "with very little disturbance."

"We rowed hard for shore," Welch continued, "hitting many salmon with our oars as we moved in, and it again appeared this time about 100 yards astern." It was swimming faster than they could row and was gaining on them.

No body-wake was visible when the animal swam. Once more it submerged and they did not see it after that.

The animal had a long neck, 6-8 feet of it protruding above the water. The neck was about the size of a stovepipe, tapering from a 20-inch diameter at the base to 8-10 inches at the head. The head was somewhat like a giraffe's; they saw it well as the creature looked up and down Johnstone Strait, turning its head this way and that. Welch noticed two bumps on the head, about 5 inches high and rounded on top. Nostrils were plainly visible, but the eyes were hard to see. No mane or hair of any sort was visible. The animal was brown in colour.[10]

Another respondent to the Leblond and Sibert survey was Cyril G. Cook, of Surrey, B.C., who reported that on a clear morning in May 1922 he and J. Philips were standing on the deck of the latter's

---

10. LeBlond and Sibert, 1973

boat, anchored near the Pulteney Point lighthouse on Malcolm Island, B.C.. It was windy and the sea was rough, with waves coming in from the northwest. "We were on stand-by," Cook wrote, "keeping a look-out for the lighthouse tender who had not yet returned to the lighthouse when I saw what I thought was the boat coming in our direction. I called to my companion that the tender was coming but did not have its sail up. We saw what we thought was the mast, but as the creature came closer we could see that it was its head and neck out of the water. We were really frightened by what we saw and breathed a sigh of relief when it kept on going— although it had a most gentle appearance and had eyes similar to those of a cow and seemed to have a film over them."

The animal seen by Cook and Philips off Malcolm Island in May 1922. (From LeBlond and Sibert, 1973) (Photo: Artwork Cook and Philips. Authors' file)

The animal swam within about 100 feet from the boat and about 300 feet offshore. Cook estimated its length at about 25 feet; the neck stuck out of the water about 7 feet, about a foot wide. The creature was brown in color, with a "scaly appearance." Mouth and nostrils were visible and the observers were struck by its large timid eyes.[11]

---

11. LeBlond and Sibert, 1973

Another encounter involving many witnesses occurred in 1932 further south, on the Sechelt coast of the Strait of Georgia. Years after the fact, writer Hubert Evans and his friends Dick Reeve and Bob Stephens, revealed that they had met with a sea-serpent off Roberts Creek. They first saw a series of bumps appear in the water, silhouetted against the setting sun. Then a shaft emerged until it was six to eight feet out of the water. The thought that the object was a log was soon dismissed: "...as we stood watching, none of us breathing a word, the top end of this shaft began to elongate horizontally until we were presented with the profile of a head, very much like a horse's in general shape, with eye bumps, nostrils, and something in the way of ears or horns. The neighbor down the way said it had stuff hanging down like hair, but I didn' t see that ," wrote Evans.[12]

Those few reports by experienced mariners would by themselves suffice to make a "prima facie" case for the presence of a large unknown animal in BC coastal waters. Because such encounters took place in different areas and usually received little if any press coverage, witnesses were isolated from each other and usually ignorant of sightings other than their own. The existence of such creature(s) remained at the level of "sailors' tales," a situation that was soon to change radically.

12. H. White, *Raincoast Chronicles* Six/Ten, pp. 276-278

Chapter 3

Front Page News

Perhaps it was a slow afternoon at the Victoria Daily Times when city editor Archie Wills heard the news. Prominent Victoria citizens were said to have seen a large sea serpent in nearby waters. It was October 1933 and the *Times* was competing for readership with the venerable Colonist. Wills immediately saw a golden opportunity to boost circulation. After all, if it was fashionable for the London press of the day to take an interest in the Loch Ness monster, why shouldn't colonial newspapers be allowed to follow suit?* Wills was a newspaper man, not a zoologist, not even a cryptozoologist, but his decision to publicize these sightings had a dramatic and long-lasting influence on Caddy's reputation.

Yachtsmen Tell of Huge Sea Serpent Seen Off Victoria

Major W. H. Langley and F. W. Kemp Describe Sighting Unusual Creature

Monster Seen on Two Different Occasions; Both Descriptions Identical

Front page headline, *Victoria Daily Times,* Oct. 5, 1933. (Photo: Authors' file)

*On May 2, 1933, a report by Alex Campbell in the Inverness Courier launched Nessie's career, soon to be prominently featured in the metropolitan press.

Next to reports of the Spanish Civil War and of Japanese attacks in northern China, the *Times* announced the encounter with a "huge sea-serpent" on the front page of its October 5, 1933 issue, specifying that "a giant sea-serpent, described as nearly eighty feet long and about as wide as the average automobile, was seen last Sunday near Chatham Island."[1] The article went on to describe the sightings in some detail.

The character of the witnesses, Major W. H. Langley, barrister and clerk of the provincial Legislative Assembly, and his wife, and Mr. F. W. Kemp, an employee of the Provincial Archives, with his family, spoke well for their credibility. While the Langleys' sighting that triggered the report had just occurred on the previous Sunday, the Kemp family encounter had taken place a year earlier, in August 1932. However, "Mr. Kemp had said nothing about seeing it last year fearing he might be ridiculed,"and would probably have gone on nursing his secret if he hadn't met with Major Langley.

On August 10, 1932, the Kemp family was spending the day on Chatham Island, when Mrs. Kemp saw a commotion in the water which threw a wash against the rocks similar to that caused by a motorboat. They saw "a mysterious something coming through the channel." In his signed statement, Mr. Kemp reports that they observed with astonishment:

A huge creature with head out of the water traveling at four miles an hour against the tide. Even at that [low] speed, a considerable wash was thrown on the rocks, which gave me the impression that it was much more reptile than serpent to make such a displacement.

The channel at this point is about 500 yards wide. Swimming to the steep rocks of the island opposite, the creature shot its head out of the water on to the rocks, and moving its head from side to side, appeared to be taking its bearings. Then fold after fold of its body came to the surface. Towards the tail it appeared serrated, like the cutting edge of a saw, with something moving flail-like at the extreme end. The movements were like those of a crocodile.

1. *Victoria Daily Times,* 5 Oct 1933, page 1. All quotes about the Kemp and Langley sighting from the same source.

Around the head appeared a sort of mane, which drifted round the body like kelp... After staying for two or three minutes, the animal slid off the rock and went on its way down the channel thrashing the water into a lather with its tail. The sun glistening on its body clearly showed its colour to be a greenish brown."

Kemp made estimates of the creature's size by measuring logs on the shore where it had briefly beached itself. The animal was considerably longer than one 60-foot long log. He also put a newspaper on the spot where it had laid its head and observed it from their original vantage point. "The animal's head was very much larger than the double sheet of newspaper. The body must have been at least five feet thick." As to the head, he thought it was oval shaped; he could not distinguish any other features, "but it was much thicker than the body."

As to the Langleys, they had been sailing slowly and silently in their Yacht Dorothy[2] on a beautiful sunny day, Sunday, October 1, 1933. It was about 1:30 p.m. when they heard "a very loud and remarkable noise, something between a grunt and a snort accompanied by a huge hiss." They saw "a huge object, 90 to 100 feet off, a little on the port bow, and on the edge of the kelp bed just off the Chatham Island shore." Although they saw the creature only for a few seconds, and concluded that they had only seen a huge dome of what was apparently a portion of its back, they agreed that "it was every bit as big as the back of a large whale but entirely different in many respects. Its colour was of a greenish brown... It had markings along the top and sides. It seemed to be of a serrated nature."

Mr. Langley added that he had been "whaling on the West Coast in 1911" and was familiar with humpback, sulphur bottom, finback and sperm whales. "There was no similarity except in size between any of these and the creature we saw on Sunday. Just shortly after it went down," continued Mr. Langley, "a swirl appeared on the surface of the water ahead of the Dorothy. My wife saw it break water a very short time afterwards on the other side of the Fulford reef.

---

2. Dorothy, considered the oldest registered sailing yacht on the BC coast is now a major artifact in the Maritime Museum of BC's collection. http://mmbc.bc.ca/collections/our-fleet-2/

The appearance was exactly similar but it was much further away and had traveled fast."

Although the descriptions provided by Kemp and Langley differ in detail, the latter wrote that: "Upon comparing notes with Mr. Kemp, the appearance of this object tallies almost exactly with the creature that he and others saw about a year ago in the same neighborhood."

The two had indeed compared notes in Archie Wills' office, signed statements and been convinced to allow them as well as their names to be published. An interpretation of the Kemp sighting was prepared by an artist for the *Times* and published shortly afterwards.

A sketch of the Kemp family 1932 sighting (*Victoria Daily Times*, 20 Oct. 1933) (Photo: Public domain)

It is interesting to note that "Mr. Kemp, who had spent a considerable part of his life on the sea, stated that monsters similar to this had been seen before in northern waters [as we described earlier], and was inclined to believe that other yachtsmen may have seen the monster which he saw." The *Times* article concluded with an invitation to its readers to provide more information on the subject.

It didn't take long for witnesses to come out of the closet! The very next day, a front-page headline proclaimed that "More People Tell Of Seeing Serpent In Sea Near Here."[3] A Captain A. M. Davies, related his encounter with a huge sea-serpent off San Diego about

---

3. *Victoria Daily Times,* Oct 6, 1933, page 1

twenty years before. It was "fighting with a whale. The serpent had wound its body around the whale twice, and as we neared it stuck its head and part of its body about thirty feet out of the water and calmly surveyed our approaching ship." Also, a Mrs. Dorothea Hooper reported to Wills that about a week before the Langley sighting she had observed a similar animal cavorting in the middle of Cadboro Bay.[4]

On October 6, Wills asked for suggestions from the *Times* readers so that "it will not be necessary to describe it as a 'weird creature' or 'an unknown denizen of the deep.' "Responses came in quickly. On October 11, Wills reported that "several suggestions for names for the monster have been received by the *Times,* one of which is 'Cadborosaurus,' which can be shortened to 'Caddy' in honor of Cadboro Bay."

The Victoria area, where many Caddy sightings occurred. (Photo: Authors' file)

---

4. *Victoria Daily Times,* Oct. 24, 1933, page 1

The original letter suggesting the name Cadborosaurus was somewhat tongue-in-cheek; the signer, I. Vacedun could not be traced. His address seemed to be that of a local jail, and Wills suspected that the letter might have originated from a reporter on the rival newspaper, the *Daily Colonist*.

The News Editor of
The Victoria Daily Times.

Dear Sir,

Why not Cadborosaurus as a name for our sea pet? It's only fair that the locality from which he was most often sighted and Possibly first discovered, should get the credit from Posterity when he may have retired to the limbo of the other monsters of land and sea. Besides, the name is euphonious, and, if too long, can be shortened to "Caddy" as a pet name, especially for the lucky ones who see him from the nineteenth hole at Oak Bay.

Yours truly,

I. Vacedun
Wilkinson Road, Saanich

Oct 6, 1933

British Columbians! Lift up a chorus!
To greet the arrival of Cadborosaurus!
He may have been here quite a long time before us,
But he's shy and don't stay around too long so as to bore us.
Cadborosaurus! Cadborosaurus!
Come up and see us again, you old war 'hoss![5]

So, Cadborosaurus it became. While some Seattle fishermen suggested "Old Hiaschuckaluck" (a variant of the Manhousat hiyitl'iik), that turned out to be too difficult to pronounce and Caddy easily won

---

5. From Archie Wills' scrapbook of Caddy clipping

out. We will follow local tradition in using Caddy as a generic name for every type of large northeast Pacific cryptid, but shall return to the matter in a later chapter, after hearing from the many witnesses.

Miffed perhaps for having been scooped, the Colonist was much less enthusiastic about the sea serpent news. Although it reported the Langley and Kemp encounters a day after the *Times*, it remained cool, suggesting, on October 14, that it might just be a giant conger eel.

However, on October 15, it could not resist scooping its rival with a new sighting by Charles F. Eagles, again in Cadboro Bay. The Colonist went on to propose its own name, Amy, for the sea serpent, without even mentioning Caddy or Cadborosaurus.[6] Both names were used for a short while, but Caddy quickly prevailed and the Colonist began to refer to "Amy Cadborosaurus," a member of the growing Caddy family.

The first Caddy postcard, sketched from life by Charles F. Eagles on 14 October 1933. Body approximate length 20 feet, diameter eight feet, tail 30 feet, head and neck 10 feet. Total length 60 feet. (Photo: Public domain)

Wills continued to exploit Caddy's presence and featured reports of sightings in the *Times*. Tactfully, he refrained from men-

---

6. *Victoria Daily Colonist,* 17 Oct. 1933, page 1

30

tioning it on October 15, a day on which long-distance swimmers attempted to cross Juan de Fuca Strait. On October 23, Mr. and Mrs. Bryden reported having seen Caddy near Trial Island, "a week after Major Langley." Rowing home after a day of fishing off Trial Island, they heard "a great commotion in the water." Bryden said he "distinctly saw two curved sections of the monster, which was spouting water with a gushing sound. The two humps I saw were separated by many feet of water. As I looked, the monster, which appeared to be of a dark green colour, disappeared beneath the surface."[7]

Experienced mariners are by far the most reliable witnesses of events at sea. On October 21, at the end of a long journey from New York, around the Horn, the master of the Grace Liner Santa Lucia, Captain William Prengel and his navigating officer J. Richardson encountered a strange object in the early morning mist in Juan de Fuca Strait, a few miles from Victoria Harbour. They had decided not to mention their 'apparition', but finding that everyone in Victoria was talking about Caddy, Captain Prengel told how: "My navigating officer called my attention to a big, peculiarly shaped object about 300 feet away. At first, we decided it was an upturned barge, but on further observation, we saw it moving, and moving rapidly too. It was in sight only a minute or two before it dived beneath the surface. We could only see what was probably the head of the serpent, and it looked from the bridge to be about the size of my cabin. We could see none of the after portions at all. It was rather misty at the time. It cut quite a wake and when it disappeared it left a wide area of foam, as if a giant tail had lashed the water." Prengel added that "the head seemed to be light in colour with white streaks running up and down it."[8] ...Caddy?

These many reports, often contradictory, led to lively speculation as to the nature of the animal. Wills was convinced of the existence of some unknown animal. As early as October 7, he editorialized: "There is abundant unimpeachable evidence that some strange marine monster either has its home in the Gulf of Georgia or frequently visits those waters. The detailed reports of responsible citizens of what they have seen of the stranger and its activities trans-

7. *Victoria Daily Times*, 23 Oct. 1933, page 1
8. *Victoria Daily Times*, 21 Oct. 1933, page 1

fer it from the world of fiction to that of reality." He left to others speculation as to its nature.

Contributed explanations included the giant squid "known to frequent the coasts of Newfoundland, Scandinavia and the British Isles" and "the plesiosaur, a giant marine reptile thought to have been extinct." Wills concluded, "Whatever the mammal [sic] might be—huge squid or plesiosaur—it certainly has been seen in the Gulf, and its presence reminds us that there still are more things in heaven and earth–and the sea as well–that are not dreamed of in the little two-by-four philosophy of mankind."[9]

Caddy's "godfather," Archie H. Wills (Photo: Mr. K. Wills used with permission.)

Francis Kermode, director of the Provincial Museum, expressed a "lively interest in marine apparitions."[10] British Columbia's most prominent zoologist, Dr. C. McLean Fraser, F.R.S.C., head of the Zoology Department at the University of British Columbia was of the opinion that "Until someone gets a lasso around one of these things we will never be able to get much farther. It is possible there are such things."[11] Another zoological authority, Professor Trevor Kincaid, of the University of Washington, in Seattle, was quoted as saying: "It seems strange that if such creatures do exist, one wouldn't have been captured by this time. Still, all accounts seem to tally. And that might mean something."[12] However, the absence of a specimen available for inspection, then as now, presents a major obstacle to scientific recognition.

After two weeks of animated public discussion of recent and older sightings, there emerged a view of Caddy as a real animal, of

9. *Victoria Daily Times,* 7 Oct.1933, page 2. Wills, as we noted, was definitely not a zoologist and obviously used to the word "mammal" to denote any large animal.

10. *Victoria Daily Colonist,* 18 Oct. 1933. Kermode, a taxidermist by trade, wisely refrained from stating an opinion on Caddy's zoological nature.

11. *Victoria Daily Times,* 10 Oct 1933, page 1

12. *Victoria Daily Times,* 21 Oct 1933, page 1

unspecified zoological attribution, drawn so as to embody "the various features described by many eyewitnesses into one sea serpent," the first of numerous attempts to synthesize the animal from disparate observations. A whole page of the Saturday edition of the *Times* was devoted to a discussion of what Caddy might be.[13] The creature depicted has a long, serpentine body, apparently undulating in the vertical plane. Much importance was placed to the serrations on its back, mentioned by several witnesses. The head resembles that of a horse, with mane and ears.

A first synthesis of Caddy, presented in the *Victoria Daily Times,* 21 October 1933. (Photo: Public domain)

News of the British Columbia sea serpent excited world-wide interest and put Victoria 'on the map,' to the great delight of the local Chamber of Commerce, which would become Caddy's staunchest supporter. The *New York Herald Tribune* announced the sea serpent's existence on October 6, 1933, immediately after publication of the Langley and Kemp sightings and kept its readers informed of further progress. The *Vancouver Sun* declared; "Whole Continent Intrigued by Caddy's Capers."

Following such a spectacular introduction in October 1933, Caddy has remained in the eye of the press, entered the marine folk-

---

13. *Victoria Daily Times,* 21 Oct. 1933

lore of local waters and posed a continuing challenge to zoological enquiry. Wills was well aware of the publicity value of Caddy at a time when dynamic Vancouver was gaining in worldly fame over the more stately provincial capital, pointing out that the "realization grows that Victoria has something which will bring it fame incomparably faster than the population, trade and crime figures of Vancouver."[14] In a more philosophical vein, he noted with disappointment the cynicism of his fellow citizens: "Your modern man would rather disbelieve something than believe it," he wrote. "He likes to think he is cynical and hard-boiled, whereas he is the most credulous creature ever made. When he can't understand a thing, like astronomy, or relativity, or finance, he believes anything you care to tell him, if you tell him with sufficient scientific or financial trimmings. But the trouble is he can understand a sea serpent. He can visualize it. Therefore, he disbelieves it. His disbelief flatters his vanity, makes him think he is a superior fellow. Well, it doesn't make him a superior fellow. Any fool can disbelieve in sea serpents..."[15]

To the end of his days, Wills felt proud and possessive about "his sea serpent." In 1970 he wrote: "I introduced Caddy to the world in 1933 and enjoyed being his sponsor and protector."[16] Wills' forceful presentation of the evidence forced the press, the public and scientists to seriously consider the possibility that there was perhaps a real animal, a "cryptid" in today's terms, to be discovered some day and brought to the fold of established zoology. If anyone is to be honored by having his name linked to Caddy's official description, it is undoubtedly Archie Wills. *Cadborosaurus willsi* has been proposed as Caddy's formal scientific name.[17]

14. *Victoria Daily Times,* 10 Oct. 1933, page 2
15. *Victoria Daily Times,* 11 Oct. 1933, page 4
16. Letter to Paul LeBlond, 13 May 1970
17. Bousfield and LeBlond, 1995

Chapter 4

A Growing Family

Following Caddy's featured appearance in the *Victoria Daily Times* in October 1933, a steady flow of reports were submitted to the press by witnesses no longer as concerned with being ridiculed. Such eyewitness reports, gradually adding details to Caddy's description, form the principal body of evidence for Caddy's existence and the clues to an eventual resolution of its zoological nature. Because eyewitness reports are anecdotal and depend on the observational and reporting abilities as well as biases of human observers, they are rightly given little scientific weight compared to the examination of material remains.

Given the frailty of human testimony, careful attention has to be given to the nature and circumstances of eyewitness reports. We have included in our compendium of sightings only encounters satisfying two criteria. First, there has to be no doubt that the object seen was an animal, not a floating tree trunk or a mass of seaweeds, for example. Second, the witnesses had to be certain that the animal seen could not have been some mistaken known marine creature or a series of animals such as sea lions in a row or a family of leaping dolphins.

We decided, for example, not to include a sighting by Vancouver Deputy Police Chief Harry Whelan who claimed to have seen Caddy while fishing in Vancouver Harbour in 1952. He could not tell "whether it was the head or the back of some unidentified 'underwater thing'" that he saw.[1] Similarly, we would not include the sighting described by Daniel Loxton, where not all members of his family could agree on what they had seen.[2] Professional skeptics may still find reasons to reject some of the reports that we have included in our list (Appendix 1). Nevertheless, to dismiss all eyewitness reports as merely anecdotal would just be foolish. In the absence of sufficient material evidence, one can either dogmatical-

---

1. *Vancouver Sun,* 19 April 1952
2. Loxton, D. and R. Prothero, 2013, p. 179

ly deny even the possibility of existence of undiscovered animals, or look for clues that might help resolve the mystery. In other words, engage in cryptozoological research.

"Cryptozoology,"claims one critic, "thrives on the failure to distinguish observations from conclusions."[3] We certainly deplore the fact that some cryptozoologists do jump to conclusions, and we will not discuss what Caddy might be until we have given the reader a chance to see the evidence. We are of course not impressed by the logic of those who besmirch the work of careful researchers by tarring everyone in the field with the same brush, especially when their only contribution to the discovery process consists in criticizing the work of others.

There are more than 230 entries in our list of reported sightings (Appendix 1). We cannot describe them all in detail, so have chosen to present here those where a closer look and a greater number of witnesses provide more details of appearance and behavior and a greater confidence in the report.

Caddy was still a novelty item when, early on Sunday morning, December 3, 1933, Cyril Andrews and his younger friend Norman Georgeson went out duck hunting off Gowland Head, near their home on South Pender Island. Andrews stated:

> I succeeded in shooting a 'golden eye' duck, but as I had only broken its wing, it began to swim to a kelp bed about fifty yards from shore. Seeing that I could not get the wounded bird, I sent Norman home for a small punt, five feet long. Returning, he was paddling across the bay towards me as I walked over a small rise to see if he was coming. As I looked across the water, I saw a head disappear some distance out. From where I was standing, I could plainly see the whole body of a sea monster just moving underneath the surface.
>
> Thinking I might alarm Norman, I did not draw his attention to what I saw, so he came along and picked me up at the point from which we had shot the bird. From there we paddled to the wounded bird in the kelp bed. I was sitting

---

3. ibid. p. 252

in the front of the punt ready to pick up the bird, when about ten feet away, out of the sea rose two coils. They reached a height of at least six feet above me, gradually sinking under the water again, when a head appeared. The head was that of a horse, without ears or nostrils, but its eyes were in front of its head, which was flat just like a horse.

I attracted Georgeson's attention to it and he saw one coil and the head well clear of the water. Then the whole thing except the head, which remained just out of the water, just sank. I was still only ten feet away from it, with the duck right beside the thing, when to my horror he gulped the bird down its throat. It looked at me then, its mouth wide open, and I could plainly see its teeth and tongue, which were like those of a fish. I would swear to the head being three feet long and two feet wide. When it closed its mouth, all the loose skin folded in neatly at the corners while its breathing came in short, sharp pants, like a dog after a run. At that point a number of seagulls swooped down at the creature, which snapped at them when they came too close. Shortly after, it sank below the surface.[4]

Caddy gets a free meal
SH South Pender Island - Dec 3rd/33.

Cyril Andrews and Norman Georgeson meet Caddy at South Pender Island. (From Archie Wills' scrapbook). (Photo: Public domain)

The two young men rushed ashore and contacted Justice of the Peace G.F. Parkyn, who immediately went to the location of the sighting and took down an affidavit of what they had seen. Parkyn had been there for some 10 minutes when the creature surfaced once

---

4. *Vancouver Sun,* 6 Dec. 1933, p.20

more, 20 yards from the shore, swimming away in an undulating motion. Eleven other people were now on the shore and also saw the creature .

In their description, Andrews and Georgeson noted that the creature's head resembled that of a horse, without ears, nostrils or whiskers. The tongue came to a point and its teeth were fish-like. It was grey-brown in color with a darker brown stripe running along the body slightly to one side. The animal was two feet in diameter; neither fins nor flippers were seen. Five humps protruded above the water surface, but there was no indication of serration on its back. The absence of this feature suggested a slightly different animal than that reported by Kemp and Langley. Popular speculation suggested that "Penda" Cadborosaurus, as it was soon called, might be a female of the species. No biological support for such an interpretation was ever put forward. Nevertheless, the Caddy family was growing.

Sketches of "Penda" Cadborosaurus by Cyril Andrews. (From Archie Wills' scrapbook.) (Photo: Authors' file)

Penda continued to frequent the waters of Pender Island in December. Andrews and his friends Arthur Pender and Kathleen Georgeson saw it again in Plumper Sound on December 21, 1933. On January 18, 1934, Andrews, Pender and Eileen McKay watched the animal near Bedwell Harbour, South Pender Island.[5] "We could

5. *Victoria Daily Times,* 23 Jan. 1934, p. 1

plainly see it undulating as it traveled towards Wallace Point. Apparently, it was feeding time, because it went out to the herring bed, and there we watched it for twenty-five minutes. There were sea gulls flying around it and they kept pecking at it. 'Penda' snapped at them, but did not get any that we saw."

Andrews confirmed that this was the same animal he had seen on previous occasions, with "a dark stripe along its back, and not a sign of flippers or fins. Another thing we could see was that it had a flesh-coloured face with no whiskers."

Cyril Andrews, Kathleen Georgeson, Arthur Pender.
(*Victoria Daily Times,* 23 Jan. 1934) (Photo: Public domain)

Caddy's taste for sea birds was in evidence when three Oak Bay residents, Coronel Marsh, Earl Marsh and J.W. Chilton saw a "female" Caddy (Penda) reaching and devouring a sea gull, near Trial Island.[6] A similar incident was described in great detail by Miss May Williams, who:

> Early Tuesday morning, Sept. 11, 1934, was awakened by a great commotion in the water at a point north of the Bradley-Dyne Estate, at Patricia Bay, North Saanich, and going to the bedroom window observed a sight that for a time seemed hard to comprehend. Some 300 feet away from

6. *Victoria Daily Times,* 9 Jan. 1934, p. 1. There is no indication as to why the witnesses thought the animal was a female.

"Penda" Cadborosaurus as She Gobbled a Seagull

A sketch of "Penda" Cadborosaurus reaching for a seagull (*Victoria Daily Times*, 9 Jan. 1934). (Photo: Public domain)

the window, at a point about 200 feet from the shore was a giant snake-like monster battling with a large number of black ducks that usually rest peacefully on the bay's quiet waters!

Miss Williams then glanced at her clock to ascertain the time —which was seven or eight minutes to six—in order to know how long she would be viewing this strange sight. She says that the monster was in sight for approximately 15 minutes, and that she had a very clear view of its head and four or five coils.

The head was like that of a giant snake, about twice the size of the neck, and was raised four or five feet above the water, the coils were arched similar to the common 'measuring worm' we are all familiar with, each coil being separated by about 10 feet of a submerged section, while the exposed 'coils' were about five or six feet in length, the thickness of the humps or coils, as near as could be judged, were about two to three feet, the tail not being visible, but allowing 10 feet for the tail, the serpent would approximately measure 70 to 80 feet in length. The color was dark."

The ducks finally decided to move to other parts and as

---

7. Sidney Review, 12 Sept 1934

they left the monster made off also, traveling in the direction of Saltspring Island, at an amazing speed."[7]

Lest anyone imagined that there was only one of these creatures, playing peek-a-boo one day as Caddy, the next as Penda, two were seen together on March 29, 1934 off the Victoria breakwater. At least, that's what Ingram McGavin, son of a local alderman, reported in the *Victoria Daily Times* on April 1st (!?) Another report of a "Caddy family" came from the crew of the tug Catala Chief who spotted two unidentified creatures in Stuart Channel, near Chemainus, BC on December 8, 1938. Captain William York Higgs and crew members John Shaw and George MacFarlane described two animals, one slightly larger than the other, about 40 feet long, with a head 16 inches across and a dark olive colour. They noted that their swimming motion was similar to that of a snake but with vertical as opposed to horizontal movements. [8] A few months later, not too far away, in Satellite Channel off Saltspring Island, members of a telephone company submarine cable gang were startled by the appearance of Caddy with "a son or a daugthter." Bob Gaetz, Frank Marshall and Bill Smith watched the pair for twenty minutes as they cavorted offshore. "The large one was plenty big," said Gaetz. "About fifteen feet of it stuck out of the water in two humps. I guess its total length would be around forty feet. The head was as big or bigger than that of a horse and shaped the same, although it had no ears... It snorted a couple of times, then bellowed like a cow. When it opened its mouth you could see teeth two inches long. The young one was exactly the same with a head about half the size of Caddy senior. I wouldn't have believed it myself if I hadn't seen the whole thing," Gaetz added.[9]

Caddy was reported twice in the waters near Crofton, BC in early 1937. On January 7, Captain M.A. Cornfield and two crewmen of the tugboat Solander described it as being 35 feet long with a head like a camel; 4 days later, J. Highsted and H, Dingee sighted "a mighty queer animal"in the same area. They also described it as camel-like and expanded on its mode of swimming: "First, the head would come above the surface—just the head—and it would swim along a bit that way. Then the neck would rise up—a neck about six

8. *Vancouver Province*, 8 Dec. 1938
9. *Vancouver Province*, 31 Mar. 1939

41

feet long—and finally the body would come into view. The back of it rose three feet above the surface. It had long hairs—like a donkey's hairs and just about the same colour, a sort of grey. And when it came up you could see the wet hairs flopping down on its back. All along its back was sort of serrated. We figure it was 35 feet long."[10]

Reports also came from the outer coast. In May 1935, Ucluelet troller Thomas Taylor saw a sea serpent as he was returning from the fishing banks, a few miles offshore. "At first he thought it was a huge whale asleep on the surface of the water, but being an old whaler, he knew it couldn't be a whale. Drawing closer to the creature, which appeared oblivious to his inspection, he described it in boating terms as being 'one hundred feet long, about six feet in circumference amidships and tapered toward bow and stern. The head appeared to be twice the size of a large sea lion and was dull grey in colour with stripes near the head.' As he approached the creature to investigate it further, it suddenly arched its back and raised its head, as a snake might do. This movement alone convinced him that this was no animal that he had ever known."[11]

Further up the coast, more fishermen reported an unusual animal. The seine boat Marmae, skippered by E. Clark, was cruising in search of pilchard when Sig Trelvik, who was on lookout, spotted what he thought was a log floating on the water. The boat changed course and ran within twenty five feet of the 'log,' when suddenly a long thick neck raised itself six feet above the water. The neck was surmounted by a small head with large protruding eyes, something like those of a dragonfly but on a much larger scale. The body was light brown and appeared to be of tremendous size and covered with fur or hair. Before the crew could mount a camera or a gun, the monster quickly sank to the depths.[12]

Caddy was already known on the Oregon coast as "Colossal Claude,"first seen cavorting at the mouth of the Columbia River in 1934 by the crew of the lightship stationed there. L.A Larsen, mate on the lightship described it as "about 40 feet long, with a neck about 8 ft long, a big round body, a mean looking tail and an evil,

10. Cowichan Chronicles, #2, 2004 pp 93-94

11. *Port Alberni West Coast Advocate,* 9 May 1935

12. *Port Alberni West Coast Advocate,* 15 Oct. 1936

13. Peter Cairns, in Sunday Oregonian, Sep. 24, 1967

Colossal Claude And The Sea Monsters

By Peter Cairns

"Colossal Claude" as featured in the *Sunday Oregonian,* Sept. 24, 1967. (Photo: Author's file)

snaky look to its head."[13] Claude was again in the news in 1937 when skipper Charles E. Graham of the troller *Viv* raced back to Astoria with the story of sighting "a long, hairy, tan colored creature with the head of an overgrown horse, about 40 feet long, and with a 4-feet waist measure."[14]

One of the most spectacular sightings of the pre-war years took place on the southern Oregon coast, about two miles south of Yachats and a dozen miles north of the famous sealion caves, a major tourist attraction. At that point, just south of Cape Perpetua, there is a chasm in the rocky shoreline known as The Devil's Churn. It was just after New Year's Day in January 1937. The weather was stormy, wet and windy, and the sea very rough. Bill Hunt and his wife Ila were sitting on a landing, watching the spectacular breakers, about 30 feet above sea level along the switchback trail which leads from the parking area off the coastal highway to the Churn.

They first sighted the creature about 250 feet seaward of the mouth of the Churn. It was coming directly towards shore, moving slowly without visible propelling motions. It stopped close to the entrance of the chasm, about 100 feet from the Hunts' observation

---

14. ibid.

point, and the breakers did not seem to toss it around one bit. A truck came by on the highway; the animal turned its head to look at it, then looked at the observers, then back at the truck. It then took off southwards along the coast, moving at a speed of about 25 knots. The Hunts followed on the highway in their car. At a viewpoint about a mile south of the Churn, the animal was about 300 feet off-shore. It then veered off the coast seawards. An unidentified man stopped his car at the lookout and they all watched the creature swim out to sea until they could see it no more.

The Hunts provided a sketch of the animal. It had a long neck, at least 15 feet, and a head which reminded them variously of a horse, a giraffe or a camel. A mane the colour of brown seaweed was visible on the neck all the way down to the body, which was about 6 feet across, with a ridge running along its back. Bill Hunt added that when the animal was in the trough of a wave, he glimpsed a tail, as long as the rest of the body, giving a total estimated length of 55 feet. While Hunt noticed small ears which "fluttered incessantly," his wife thought that the animal had small straight horns on its head, eight to ten inches high and "the size of a small water pipe."[15]

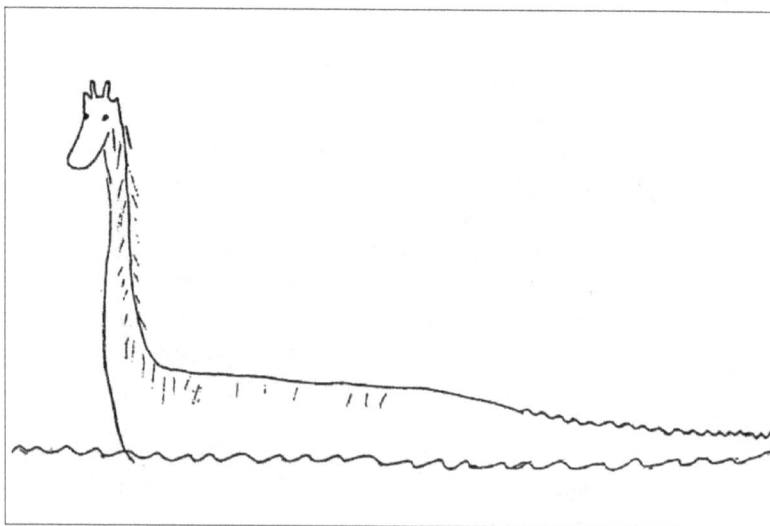

The Yachats sea serpent, as sketched by the Hunts (LeBlond & Sibert, 1973). (Photo: Authors' file)

---

15. LeBlond and Sibert, 1973

While Caddy was the focus of attention on the Pacific Coast, Ogopogo, the Lake Okanagan cryptid, had long been the subject of similar interest in the interior of British Columbia. Caddy had already been reported from the lower reaches of the Fraser River [16] and seemed to venture freely into fresh water. It's perhaps not surprising that, in spite of Archie Wills' disdain for Ogopogo, which he dismissed as "a purely fictitious sea-serpent,"[17] there was some confusion in the public mind about the two creatures, especially when seen in river waters. An extraordinary creature which appeared in the Harrison River in August 1936 was heralded as "the grand-daddy of all Ogopogos." When first seen, "it resembled in appearance the periscope of a submarine," however the description which followed in the Chilliwack Progress of three separate one-hundred-foot long parts joining together leaves one quite skeptical about the reality of the event or at least of the accuracy of the description.[18]

By the late 1930s, Caddy had become well established in the realm of public awareness. Eye-witness reports from California to Alaska were frequently published in the major newspapers. So well established, that the British Columbia Fisheries Department did not shy away

Sea Serpent On Islands

Victoria, Oct 18. The British Columbia fisheries department has been advised of the sighting off the Queen Charlotte Islands of a creature with a head resembling that of a horse. It is said to be about 10 feet long and resembling Victoria's celebrated Cadborosaurus or Caddie.

from publishing the following notice in the Prince Rupert *Daily News*.[19]

While zoologists did not deny the possibility of Caddy's existence, they could not, then as now, be sure until an actual specimen was available for examination. The public was generally much more positive about the likelihood of such a creature inhabiting the vast ocean. There was even some expectation of an imminent discovery

---

16. *Vancouver Sun*, 8 Jan. 1934
17. *Victoria Daily Times*, 17 Oct. 1933, p. 2
18. *Chilliwack Progress*, 26 Aug. 1936, p. 1
19. *Prince Rupert News*, 18 Oct 1937, P 1

or capture of a specimen that would settle the issue. In 1938, Dr. G. H. Worthington, President of the Vancouver Tourist Association was prepared to take advantage of Caddy's recognition: "If the sea serpent is here we'll put him in next year's publicity—but it will have to be authenticated indeed—with pictures."[20]

Unbeknownst to Dr. Worthington, a discovery made the previous year at the Naden Harbor whaling station, in the Queen Charlotte Islands, might have answered some questions about Caddy's nature, had the specimen received proper care and scrutiny. The story of the Naden Harbor carcass is presented in a later chapter.

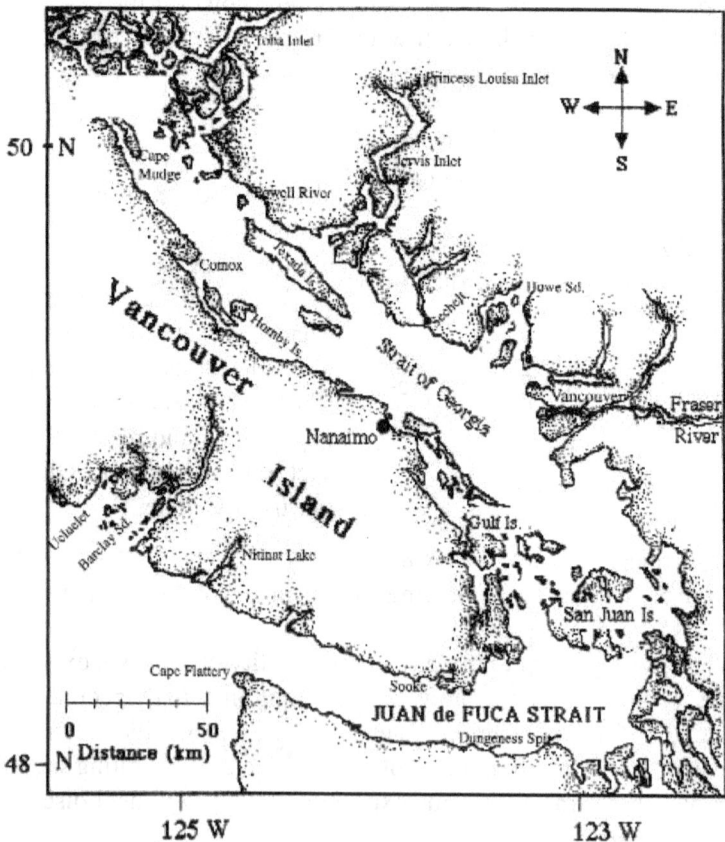

The Strait of Georgia: Caddy's playground. (Photo: Authors' file)

---

20. *Victoria Daily Times* 12 Aug. 1938, p. 1

Chapter 5

A Beast of Many Colours

Occasionally and unpredictably, Caddy continues to show up along the northeast Pacific coast, from California to Alaska. Each sighting brings out details at once revealing and confusing. Appendix 1 presents a complete list of sightings, with salient details. We only present the most informative of these sightings, drawing the reader's attention to important features of the appearance and behavior of the beast. The incidents presented are not in chronological order. They are arranged as to their significance or importance in the study of Caddy.

Many encounters have taken place in the waters near Victoria, where a busy port and the proximity of a Canadian Navy base make for very active marine traffic. An officer from the Navy base in Esquimalt, out fishing in a row-boat, had a close look at Caddy. Lieutenant Commander X (the *Victoria Daily Times* knew the officer's name but agreed not to publish it) was fishing from an open boat on a sunny afternoon in November 1950, about a third of a mile from the mouth of Esquimalt Harbour, between McCauley and Brothers Islands. There was a heavy swell and a stiff breeze, but visibility was excellent. The lure was 70 feet out behind the boat and Caddy crossed astern, between the boat and the lure. "He was 30 feet from head to tail and created a heavy wash," said the officer."

Navy officer encounters Caddy while fishing (From Archie Wills' scrapbook) (Photo: Artwork: A. Payne/Authors' file)

He surfaced about every 35 feet. Each time, he lifted his head from the water he opened his mouth wide and showed two rows of large teeth which has a saw-tooth appearance. Before he dove he snapped his teeth together with a terrifying sound."[1]

For 25 seconds, Lieutenant Commander X had a good look at Caddy. Its head was something like that of an ordinary garden snake, about 18 inches across and two feet in length. The eyes were jet black, two to three inches in diameter. The neck was about six feet long, and where it joined the body, there was a widening, as of shoulders. It propelled itself with large flippers on either side and its enormous tail appeared flat like that of a beaver. Caddy's body had a gradual hump but in no part was it serrated. No gills were visible in the head. The head and body were covered with hair, brown in colour. "I don't mind admitting that I was terrified," said the officer, "especially when it snapped its jaws." We note however that a sketch of the encounter departs in some points from the verbal description, showing a serrated back and many humps.

Dungeness Spit is a long finger of sand that juts out into Juan de Fuca Strait, near the entrance to Puget Sound, across from Victoria. It is an exhilarating place for a seaside stroll. On a clear day, the mountains of Vancouver Island are visible to the north; snow-capped volcanic Mt. Baker towers to the east. On a mid-March afternoon, in 1961, Margaret Stout and her sister-in-law Mrs. Fred Parsons were walking along the spit with their young sons, aged four and five. Mrs. Stout reported:

> It was a dark, drizzly and quiet day. We could see Vancouver Island through the mist. Ships in the channel were easily visible. We were at the beginning [western end] of the spit. We were watching a large freighter far out in the channel. It was moving up the Strait towards Port Townsend. When it was about 45° northeast of us, our attention was drawn to a long thin object about 25° northeast and probably a quarter of a mile away from us. At first, we thought it was a tree limb. It disappeared abruptly beneath the surface and in a few seconds appeared again, much closer. We could see that it was some kind of creature and distinctly saw that the large flattish head was turned

---

1. Letter to Archie Wills

away from us and towards the ship. I think all of us gasped and pointed. We could distinctly see three humps behind the long neck. The animal was proceeding westward at an angle towards us. It sank abruptly again and reappeared closer, almost due north of us.

In the dim light, we could distinctly make out color and pattern, a long floppy mane, and the shape of the head. My small son grabbed me and started to cry with fear. At the same time, the animal seemed to become aware of us and sank again. It reappeared again in a few seconds, still proceeding westwards, but a little way from us. I reassured the youngster, saying that it was obviously wary of us. It sank and reappeared once more while near enough to observe it closely. My sister-in-law is a good photographer and had her 35 mm camera. We had time to discuss that she should try to get a picture of it. She said the light was too poor and the background of the dull sea would not give any contrast. Mostly we were so busy exchanging notes and keeping track of the creature's progress that there was not time.

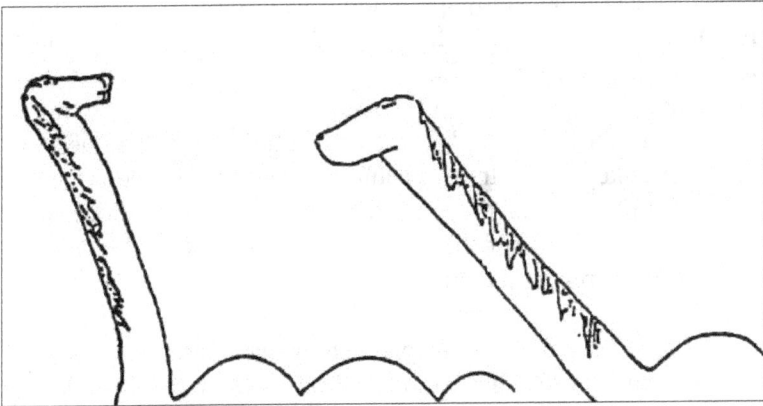

Two views of Caddy, as seen by Margaret Stout from Dungeness Spit. From Leblond and Sibert, 1973. (Photo: Authors' file)

We estimated that the length of the exposed neck was at least six feet and the head at least twenty inches long. As a trained biologist," added Mrs. Stout, "including marine and fresh water biology, I could not accept that long floppy mane or fin. Yet we all saw it. It was a limply hanging thing.

We deduced that the humps were at least five feet. Again, I could not accept their arrangement. They were close together without visible curve. If it had not been for the humps, we would have said it resembled pictures of the herbivorous marsh-living dinosaurs. The animal was a rich deep brown with large reticulations of a bright, burnt orange. The pattern wasn't unlike that of a giraffe except much larger.

We could see no body movements except that the neck lowered and moved backward with grace and the head swiveled, raised and lowered. Its forward progression was smooth, like a swan's. It sank and rose almost perpendicularly; although there was no indication of effort, it progressed westward, toward Port Angeles, at a fair rate of speed. The whole episode lasting about eight minutes.[2]

Quite conscious of the unusual nature of the encounter, Mrs. Stout reflected: "My sister-in-law is almost militantly prosaic, refusing to accept almost any explanation for phenomena, experienced by others or even herself, that are not well established and common. I, on the other hand, enjoy speculation and discussion about subjects not necessarily verified by factual evidence. Even so, I think that I am an objective witness. The reactions in both small boys, without any promptings, to me was reinforcement to we adults accepting the evidence of our own eyes." There can be little doubt that these two somewhat skeptical witnesses actually saw what they described.

Crossing back to the Canadian side of Juan de Fuca Strait, David Miller who was fishing near the Discovery Island lighthouse, near Victoria, reported that:

While engaged in commercial fishing one afternoon , in late November 1959, my partner Alfred Webb and I observed this strange creature surface roughly 80 feet on our port beam. It started to move rapidly away from us so we speeded the engine up and gave chase. We got within 30 feet when it suddenly submerged, not in the method seals and sealions do but as though something pulled it under. A few minutes later we arrived at its place of submergence and

---

2. LeBlond and Sibert, 1973

there was a tremendous turbulence suggesting a creature the size of a 30-foot sei whale. Its speed under was also astounding as it surfaced a few minutes later over a hundred yards away. It stayed up while we took off after it again but this time it never let us get close again.

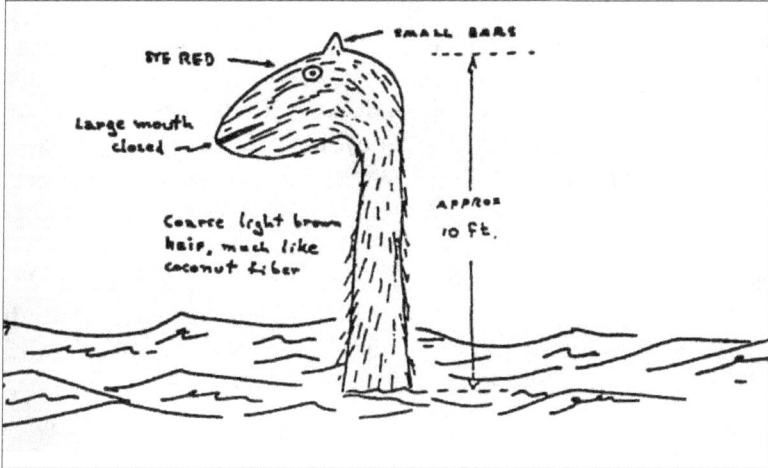

The creature seen by David Miller and Alfred Webb, off Discovery Island. (LeBlond and Sibert, 1973). (Photo: Authors' file)

The first encounter was so close that both of us remarked about its large red eyes and short ears visible at that range. Both of us have commercially fished on this coast since we were small boys and have observed on many occasions groups of sea lions and seal traveling to new grounds and to the unlearned do resemble something odd especially when the bull rears up, followed by several females. I have also observed elephant seals offshore and they look strange but not like this creature. Other fishermen friends of mine have also reported strange creatures much resembling the one we saw but are reluctant to report it to the papers or authorities because of the usual ridicule which follows such sightings."[3]

Again, we have competent witnesses familiar with sea creatures. There is no reason to believe that what they reported is not

---

3. LeBlond and Sibert, 1973

what they saw. It's also of some interest that they did not claim "to have seen Caddy"; they report an unusual creature and do not appear to be riding on the coat-tails of a well-publicized news story.

Sketches drawn by eye-witnesses are of course not photographic reproductions; they are limited in their fidelity of description by the biases as well as by the ability of the observer to draw what they think they see. When Mrs. M. Tildesley and her friend Mr. Duncalfe sat on the beach at Ten Mile Point, near Victoria, sketching the Olympic Mountains across Juan de Fuca Strait, these two skilled artists both watched Caddy swim by. It was a clear and very calm day in the summer of 1939. They were having lunch, at about 1:30 pm, when Duncalfe suddenly shouted "Caddy. "About 100 feet from shore there appeared what looked like a long greenish-yellow log moving very fast westwards. The creature dived "hardly disturbing the water" and came up again further out going towards Cadboro Bay. They lost sight of it around the headland. Mrs. Tildesley guessed the length of the neck at 6–10 feet. No other part of the body was visible. The head was small and hardly distinguishable from the neck.[4]

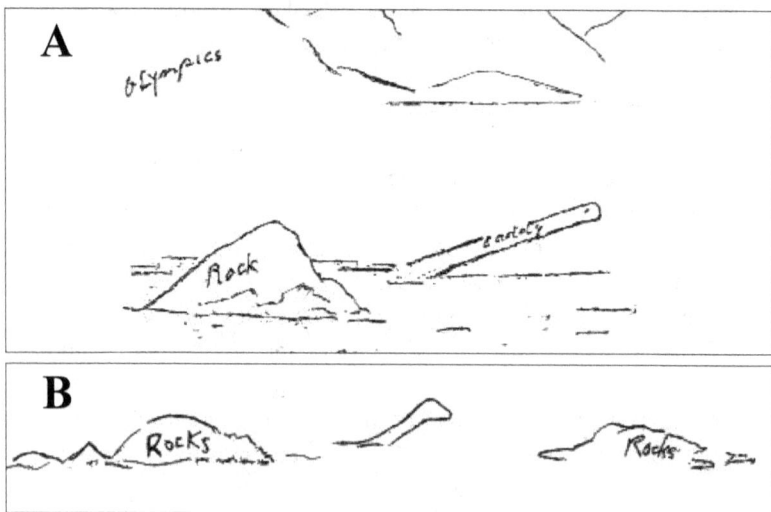

Caddy as seen and sketched by Mrs. Tildesley (A) and Mr Duncalfe (B) who saw it together in the summer of 1939. (From LeBlond and Sibert, 1973). (Photo: Authors' file)

---

4. LeBlond and Sibert, 1973

Mrs. Tildesley sent a sketch with her report, received in 1969, in response to the general enquiry sent out by LeBlond and Sibert, who suggested she contact Mr. Duncalfe, by then an art teacher in Brooklyn, N.Y. The two sketches, drawn well after the fact, unfortunately show little detail, but some difference in the shape of the head.

Artist and photographer Wilfred Gibson watched Caddy from his home in Mill Bay, and saw it snatch at seabirds. The silhouette sketch that he contributed shows few details but illustrates a by-now familiar behaviour.[5]

Caddy snatching at birds; sketch by Wilfred Gibson. (Photo: Public domain)

Caddy also showed up near Vancouver. Vancouver restaurateur Peter Pantages, his wife Helen, and a friend, Chris Altman, spotted it when fishing in English Bay, "somewhere between the bell buoy and Siwash Rock, in 1947. According to Mr. Pantages, the animal had a horse's face and three humps. It swam up and down like a caterpillar. Its skin was dark, but not as dark as that of a ' blackfish' (a pilot whale). Both Mrs. Pantages and Mr. Altman noticed the large eyes; they also heard the animal snort as it blew water through its nose."[6] Caddy was also known as 'Sarah the Sea Hag' in Vancouver and was seen in the outer harbour, near the Point Grey bell buoy by Frank McPhelan in May 1947. "Believe me, it was big and it was alive," he said, "about twenty feet long and a big coil above the surface."[7]

---

5. *Vancouver Province,* 14 Jan. 1943
6. Letter and telephone conversation with P.H. LeBlond, July 1971
7. *Seattle Post-Intelligencer,* 19 May 1947

Further out in Vancouver's outer harbour, on a bright sunny morning in January 1984, mechanical engineer Jim N. Thompson was fishing for salmon in his motorized Folbot kayak. He was about 200 yards north of the most westerly Spanish Banks channel marker, in calm seas. Glancing south towards the mouth of the Fraser River, he saw for five to ten seconds a furry, somewhat serpent-like creature about 100 feet away.

It surfaced in the trough of a swell and looked back at me, while moving westward very fast. It appeared to be 18-20 feet long with a craned neck and a smallish camel or giraffe-like head pointed in my direction. I discounted its being a sea-otter swimming on its back. Definitely furry-at least at the head end anyway—and was gliding in an up-and-down swimming motion at an estimated 15–20 mph. It submerged into a crest and I did not see it again. I never mentioned it to anyone-not even to my wife who may have poo-pooed it anyway. It was 22–26 inches wide; 4 ft emerged from the water. It was whitish tan in colour on the throat & lower front to a solid tan upper head. It has small horns; giraffe-like stubs; and what appeared to be large floppy ears, with one bent forward over the forehead. Eyes and mouth were clearly visible.[8]

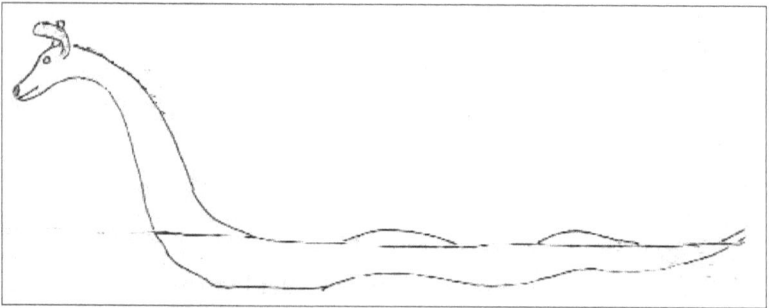

Jim Thompson's sketch of Caddy off Spanish Banks, Vancouver. (Photo: Authors' file)

Observant readers will have noticed that besides some commonly recurring features (long neck, horse-like head...) eye-wit-

---

8. Letter to P.H. LeBlond, 22 July 1985

nesses describe other often different colour (varying from dark to yellow to grey to blue) and even contradictory features (horns or ears, a mane, hairless or furry skin...). Even a pair of artists, Tildesley and Duncalfe, viewing the same animal, show different head shapes in their sketches. Whether differences between various descriptions reflect actual differences in the animals seen or are merely a result of personal impressions, observational skills and sketching abilities is of course a matter of great interest in interpreting witnesses' descriptions.

Bill Hunt, for example, at the Devil's Churn, saw small ears which "fluttered incessantly," while his wife saw "small straight horns." Miller and Webb described small ears while Jim Thompson saw ears as well as horns. Cyril Andrews had a close look; he mentioned the absence of ears. One who saw horns was Roy Duesenbury, of Blakeley Island (near Pender Island, BC) who was working on his wood pile at mid-morning in November 1940 when he heard a sound like a rush of wind. "The monstrosity had a head like a horse with two horns, which were blunt." The neck appeared to be short, but the whole animal was about 40 feet long.[9]

Sointula fisherman N. Erickson definitely saw ears. He was heading home from Vancouver when he saw an unfamiliar creature near the Merry Island lighthouse, in the Strait of Georgia. The sea was calm, the weather clear and the sun was about to set, at 8:00 p.m. on July 7, 1957.

I noticed this object in my course of traveling that I thought was a three-foot driftwood, but getting closer I noticed splashing at one end which I thought was a duck trying to climb on this driftwood. Getting closer then I noticed like big nostrils at the other end and the splashing was that it was flipping his ears. It was only the head on the surface, so I got as close as 20 yards and it just submerged and disappeared. After I ran over him he came to the surface just 15 feet behind the boat and then turned my way and did not appear afraid of being so close. This time he came up so I could see two humps on his back.

9. *Vancouver Province,* 19 Nov. 1940

The animal was brown in colour, it had no mane in spite of its equine appearance, but very short fur. Ears, eyes, mouth and nostrils (big and round, bigger than a horse's) were visible. It was about 12 feet long and 4 feet wide with two humps on its back.[10]

Caddy is a fast swimmer. Many observers have expressed amazement at its speed. A striking demonstration of its abilities involves a pair of individuals seen swimming together in Saanich Inlet in the summer of 1993. Sea-plane pilots James Wells and Don Berends of Cooper Air Services were prac-

The animal seen by N. Erickson: a) first glance; b) after going "over it," more of the body emerging. (Photo: Authors' file)

ticing water landings in Brentwood Bay when they spotted what they first took for two large fish or seals just ahead as they landed. On taxiing closer, they noted that both creatures were much larger than seals or fish. Each had two shallow vertical humps, or coils, in tandem above the water surface, under which they could see about six inches of daylight. Each hump was three to four feet in length, one foot to 16 inches thick; the humps were about five to eight feet apart, in tandem for a total length of 12 to 14 feet from the beginning of the first hump to the end of the second. The pilots did not see a head or a tail in either animal. They could not catch up with them at taxiing speeds of up to 40 mph![11]

Caddy makes noises. Gaetz and companions who saw a pair of them in Satellite Channel heard the larger one "bellow like a cow." Arthur Dawe had a good look at Caddy through binoculars from his home on Cadboro Bay. "It had something of a camel's head and three distinct undulations. It would dive and then come to the surface and 'blow.' When I heard the blow I thought it might be a

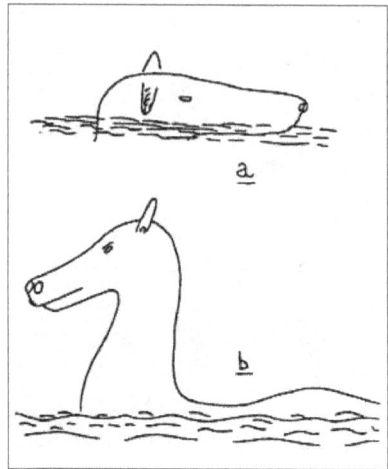

10. LeBlond and Sibert, 1973
11. *Victoria Times-Colonist,* 28 July 1993, p.1

blackfish (pilot whale) and I studied it closer, but it was no black-fish and it wasn't a porpoise or a sea lion. It seemed to be feeding and stayed off our place for five minutes. Then it dove and disappeared."[12]

Caddy has even been reported on shore! The animal seen by the Kemp family in 1932 beached itself briefly on Chatham Island. In 1936, E.J. Stephenson, together with his wife and son, watched a 90-foot long, three-foot-thick animal wriggling over the reef into a lagoon on Saturna Island. The animal was yellow and bluish in colour.[13] In a sudden and frightening encounter in June 1991, Sidney resident Terry Osland came face to face with a large unknown creature at the beach near Ardmore Point, Saanich Inlet. Her dog, Lady, was pulling on the leash, reluctant to go forward, when they came in sight of the beach. Then, as Mrs. Osland described to Patrick Murphy of the *Times Colonist:*

"I saw this face looking at me, then it disappeared over the edge and the dog was fighting to get away. I heard a splash and I looked over and saw the back end go into the water. It then came up twice and I saw the top of its head. It was bigger than a killer whale. I've seen them, and it couldn't have been an elephant seal. It was hard to describe. It was smooth, it had no hair and the tail was rounded like a lizard tail and it had like little feet on the side back of the tail. It had grey, silvery colour skin that resembled the smooth skin of a dog fish. I never saw a long neck."[14]

One of the most unusual sighting on record was reported by Charles Dudoward, of Port Simpson, BC (now Lax Kw'alaams) in response to the LeBlond and Sibert 1969 survey; it describes a "two-headed monster. "His letter of November 29, 1969 speaks of an event "some 25 years ago," in the 1940s. Fishermen Fred Dudoward (Charles' brother), Bud Helme and a Mr. Ivarson, each in his own boat, were fishing near Finlayson Island. Dudoward heard "a whistling noise and found himself facing a double-headed mon-

---

12. *Vancouver Province,* 17 April 1936, p.1
13. Advance, Langley, BC. 22 Apr. 1960, p.1
14. Victoria Times-Colonist , 31 Jul. 1993, p.1

ster 100 yards away." He immediately cut his lines and ran home. The other two fishermen followed close behind, abandoning their nets.

"It really had two heads,"Fred Dudoward added, "joined together and two lumps appeared behind. It dived under water, just the two heads, leaving the two lumps still out of the water. Every time the two heads are out of the water, it blew a spray of water like steam and whistled like a hot bearing." The colour was brownish and there was no hair but the skin was shiny like that of a porpoise or a whale. The witnesses did not remember seeing any ears. The two heads were "like a beaver's head but a tremendous size, uglier and wicked." The accompanying sketch was drawn under the witnesses' guidance... after 24 iterations, they agreed that a true likeness had been reached.[15]

The 'two-headed' monster described by Charles Dudoward (LeBlond and Sibert, 1973). (Photo: Authors' file)

Although they recognized that the fishermen would have been expected to be familiar with all kinds of whales seen on the BC coast, LeBlond and Sibert dismissed the report as being most likely a pair of whales swimming in unison, as suggested by the "blowing of water,"the hairless skin and the small "wicked eyes." We have retained this report because there is a striking similarity between Dudoward's description and that of the closely swimming pod of animals more recently reported and photographed by Nash (Chapter 8). Quite possibly Dudoward's report relates to a pair of animals

---

15. LeBlond and Sibert, 1973

swimming closely enough to confuse observers. Perhaps the description of a three-headed creature sighted by Chet and Rose Charlton in Qualicum Bay, Vancouver Island, in April 1951 also reflects the presence of three animals swimming in unison. "We could see the big teeth and red linings of the mouths. The necks were 12–18 inches thick and were covered with wrinkled folds of flesh or blubber. It was definitely all one unit with no visible breaks," the Charltons insisted. Further, "the monster could be heard wheezing each time it surfaced for air."[16]

Another noisy breather and blower was seen by Kaye Hanson. Rowing her canoe near North Harwood Island in 1947, she saw "a head and big neck 3 feet out of the water and two bumps approximately 12 feet apart. The head would dip and submerge, followed by the bumps, then the head would reappear and then again followed by the bumps in an up and down motion."[17] She heard a blowing sound each time the head area emerged and saw spray from the head area...perhaps from the mouth(?). There is also evidence of "blowing" in Nash's report.

Kaye Hanson's "blowing" Caddy. (Photo: Authors' file)

16. Vancouver Sun, 3 Apr. 1951
17. Report to Jason Walton

Chapter 6

Back in the Limelight

Following publication in 1995 of an earlier version of this book[1] accompanied by a formal zoological description,[2] there was a renewal of public interest in Caddy, especially among younger people and among the many recent newcomers to the Pacific coast, many of whom had never heard of it before. Numerous reports of new sightings as well as memories of older encounters were brought to our attention. They are included in the list of sightings in Appendix 1.

The wide dissemination of sketches provided by earlier witnesses created a basis for describing newly observed unfamiliar creatures. Many reports mentioned a similarity with previous observations. Others emphasized the differences.

Scott McNeill, for example, was on his way to work on a bright sunny morning in 1993, riding the ferry from Gabriola Island to Nanaimo when he saw what he assumed at first to be a pod of sealions, traveling very close, in a line. Upon closer approach, when a single head raised itself above the water and "nonchalantly" looked at the ferry, he realized that he was looking at a single animal. "It was definitely not camel or horse-like," he specified. "It had a round small head, no bigger than its neck, sort of like a brontosaurus but not as blunt. Its eyes were looking forward, like a dog. Also, the creature I saw had no mane on its neck nor did it have any visible protuberances at all from its head, along its neck and back. Completely smooth. No visible whiskers, teeth or beard. Its skin was dark brown and smooth."

McNeill did not send in a sketch, but left us a remarkably detailed description. "The head was mounted on a long neck that I was only able to see when it lifted its head above water... the neck was the same thickness as the head." He also provided estimates of dimensions: "From the tip of its nose to where the first hump entered the water, about 8–10 feet. From the front of where the first

---

1. LeBlond and Bousfield, 1995
2. Bousfield and LeBlond, 1995

of more than 3 humps entered the water and to the rear of the last hump was about 25–35 feet. The largest middle hump rose to a height of about 2–2.5 feet and was about 6 feet long. "Further, he "thought long and hard of a good analogy" for the motion of the creature: "Picture a side view cut-away of a 5 cylinder in-line motor," he wrote, "As the end pistons and middle piston go up and down, so the two in-between go the opposite way. Add to that motion the rolling effect (or porpoising), like a whale or seal, through the water, as opposed to pushing/displacing the water as in a boat or a duck. This action is very slow and rhythmic and leaves an extremely small wake. It seems to propel the animal very easily at about 5 miles an hour."[3]

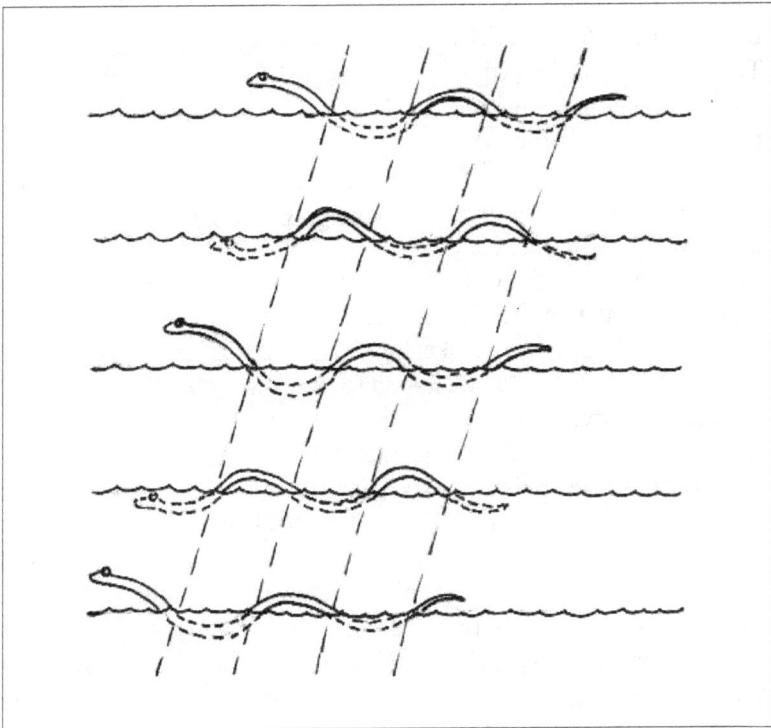

Scott McNeill's interpretation of Caddy's swimming motion. This kind of swimming is also evident in Kelly Nash's video discussed in a later chapter. (Photo: Author's file)

---

3. E-mail to Paul LeBlond, 26 Oct. 2001

Caddy continues to turn up in its familiar Salish Sea haunts, an area so named after the local First Nations and including Juan de Fuca Strait, the Strait of Georgia and Puget Sound. In July 1994, David Holt, an experienced wildlife cruise leader, saw "a large head and neck that rose vertically, remained for 40 seconds and then sank" in Roberts Bay, Sidney, BC. The animal was approximately 10 feet in height and blackish green in colour (sea lion tone). Five passengers saw it too. One of them described it as "ugly."[4]

The animal seen by David Holt and passengers. (Photo: Authors' file)

In August 1995, Anita Newberry saw two huge dark brown humps, 30–50 feet from shore in Victoria, approximately 6 feet from each other, drifting like logs... She described the humps as having a gap in the middle enough to "stick your hand through..."[5] Vancouver lawyer David Harris and a group of sailing friends spotted Caddy in Howe Sound in October of that year, near Bowen Island. Harris was pointing to a seal, 100 feet off the port beam but "as we watched, the head rose on a long neck and it was clearly not a seal," he said. "The head was about 10 inches in general overall diameter. It didn't have a prominent dog muzzle shape [of a seal], but was more generally rounded like a very large fist... Suddenly the head and neck sped forward straight southbound, maintaining the same erect distance out of the water for about 15–20 feet, then it submerged and disappeared."[6] In August 1995, Jim Torrance (another lawyer) and holidaying friends, who had never heard of

---

4. Report to Jason Walton
5. Report to Jason Walton 20 May 2000
6. *Victoria Times-Colonist,* 17 Oct. 1995.

Caddy, saw an animal with a 6 foot long neck and red eye in Cordova Channel, near Victoria.[7] In January 1996, Ivor Cooke was watching naval frigates in action through his binoculars off Saxe Point, Esquimalt, as "a wedge-shaped" head emerged. "The head was like a horse but stubbier," he said. He estimated the animal as being about 15 to 30 feet long.[8] Bob Iverson watched something in the ocean from his house in Telegraph Cove in August 1998 and described the event as "big tires popping up suddenly, everywhere. Eight tire-like objects seen, not all at the same time."[9] Adele Kirwer saw a marine animal for 5–10 minutes at the mouth of Cadboro Bay in June 2011. She reported a length of more than 20 feet; it was swimming across the waves; very dark—like wet dark hair.[10]

Caddy continues to make frequent appearances in Saanich Inlet. In mid-July 1995, a woman watched through her binoculars "a big Caddy head and two humps with a smaller beast swimming along-side" in Finlayson Arm.[11] Peter Gage and his wife were riding the Mill Bay ferry on July 24, 1996 when they "saw the coil just ahead of the ferry and then it disappeared... It was eight inches thick and a foot out of the water. It was a cross between Cambridge blue and silver grey."[12]

Marjory Neal lives on the Saanich Inlet waterfront on Ardmore Drive. She saw Caddy twice in the summer of 2004. On June 8, she saw a "huge hump and I could see water on the other side through the half-circle." A few days later, on June 11, she was sitting on the deck with a friend when they both saw "a head, long neck and one huge hump following. It left quite a wake when it went under the water. Not like a whale, dolphin, seal or fish—it actually went down like a submarine."[13]

The archipelago of the Canadian southern Gulf Islands and their southern extension as the American San Juan Islands has also been

---

7. Letter to Paul LeBlond, 8 Oct. 2008
8. *Victoria Times-Colonist,* 24 Jan. 1996
9. Report to Jason Walton, 20 May 2000
10. E-mail to John Kirk, 26 July. 2011
11. *Victoria Times-Colonist,* 20 Aug. 1995
12. *Victoria Times-Colonist,* 27 July 1996
13. Letter to Paul LeBlond, July. 2008

favoured with numerous Caddy sightings. Readers will recall Cyril Andrews' dramatic encounter off Pender Island (Chapter. 4). In May 1996, Les Bachmeier was holidaying on Saltspring Island when he saw "four large glistening coils" moving steadily through Ganges Harbour. He "could see daylight under the first three... it moved as a unit and was not four separate animals." He did not see head, tail, flippers...or any other appendages.[14]

Les Bachmeier's view of Caddy in Ganges Harbour, 1996. (Photo: Authors' file)

In October 2005, Mark Drake and Kelly Woods were sitting on the rocks on the east side of Galiano Island, looking into the Strait of Georgia, when they saw "what we thought to be a slender whale or porpoise," an interpretation which lasted only a fraction of a second when they saw that the animal had a "large horse almost snake-like head... covered with a sort of matted down hairy mane which was the colour of a red retriever with dark and lighter streaks." When the creature submerged, they "observed a hump that followed the motion of the body..."[15] In nearby Active Pass, between Galiano and Mayne Islands, Lisa Lake watched Caddy swim by in the summer of 2000; tall neck, two loops and a "tail like a whip."[16]

---

14. Letter to Paul LeBlond, 23 May 1996
15. Letter to Paul LeBlond, 2 Nov. 2005
16. Letter to Paul LeBlond, 2 Aug. 2010

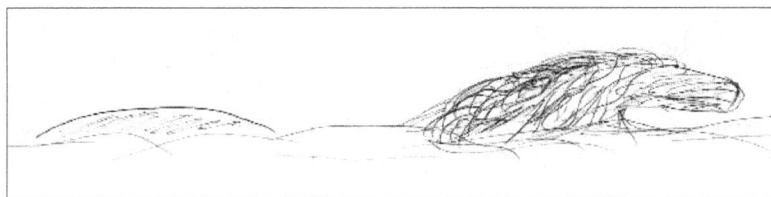

Caddy, as described by Drake and Woods, seen off Galiano Island, 2005. (Photo: Authors' file)

lisa lake
2000 .
Active Pass

Caddy swimming through Active Pass in 2000, as sketched by Lisa Lake. (Photo: Authors' file)

At the other end of Galiano Island, Alan Vittery was boating through Porlier Pass in May 2001. His party was "completely astonished (and we still are) at what we saw. Its head was 2 to 3 feet above the water and looked like the head of a giant worm. The colour was brownish and kind of slimy looking. We could see the outline of a mouth and my wife says she saw the head rotating although I can not say that for sure."[17]

---

17. E-mail to bccryptoclub, 23 May 2001

Much further south, in San Francisco Bay, the Clark brothers, Bob and Bill, reported numerous sightings of a large animal, more than 30 feet long, with four fins and a flattish snout. They provided a sketch which shows much detail of the underside, with small fins, scales and details of colouring, but unfortunately doesn't show the head.[18] The Clark brothers more recently forwarded a report of a long-necked creature seen swimming in 2008 at the south end of San Francisco Bay, near the San Mateo bridge.[19]

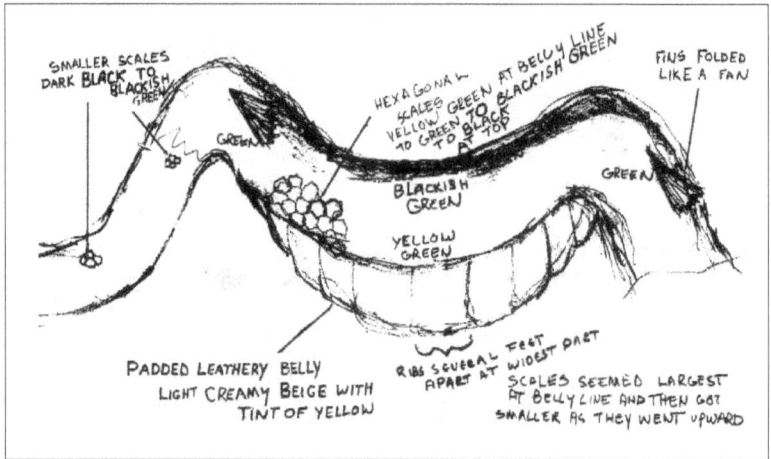

Sketch of the creature seen by the Clark brothers in San Francisco Bay. (Photo: Author's file)

Now turning to the north, one of us was fortunate enough to catch a glimpse of Caddy in the Fraser River, near its mouth at Steveston, BC. John Kirk related the encounter as follows:

> This morning at 11:45 (Aug 16, 2010) I saw an animal with its head sticking three feet out of the water as it swam majestically toward the mouth of the Fraser River near Steveston. At first I thought I was looking at Ogopogo then I realized where I was. Trailing behind the head and neck were two low humps. I could not believe my eyes. This thing—I am assuming it was a Caddy—also had what

18. Letter to Ed Bousfield, 1 Feb. 1996
19. E-mail to John Kirk, 20 Aug. 2013

looked like a mane and I swear it had ears. I know that is not supposed to be the case, but I am sure they were ears. It was heading from east to west towards the Salish Sea. Just like I have seen Ogopogo react, this animal sunk down vertically when a fast moving boat happened on the scene. I saw it again briefly, but then it was gone for good.[20]

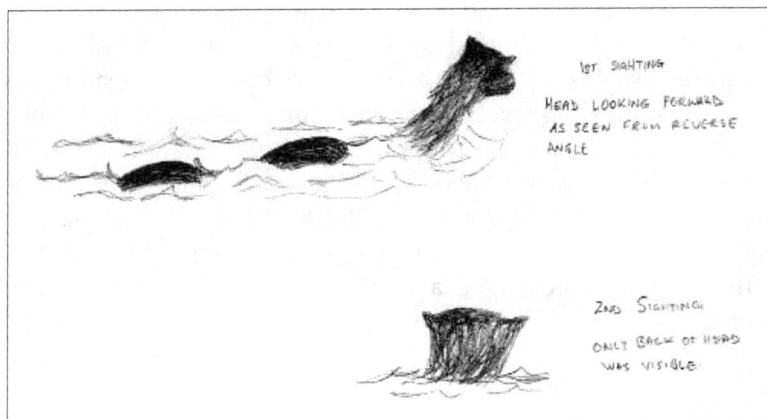

Caddy as seen by John Kirk, near the mouth of the Fraser River. (Artwork and Photo: J. Kirk)

The following summer (27 July 2011), Sunny Fung and his wife also saw a "5 feet long hump curled like a smaller version of ogopogo" in the middle arm of the Fraser River.[21]

Continuing northwards in the Strait of Georgia, we heard from Chelsea Murray, of Powell River, BC about a sighting of July 2011. Her family lives on a waterfront property in the Myrtle Point area. She and her mother were "shocked to see a creature they had never seen before... It was dark tan colour, had a large smoother head, no visible fins, but the most shocking thing was the way it moved... up and down creating semi-circles along the surface of the ocean... It moved very fast."[22]

Continuing our northward progression, we come to the waters near Denman and Hornby Islands, where on Dec 8, 2011 the

---

20. E-mail to Paul LeBlond and Jason Walton, 16 Aug. 2010
21. E-mail to John Kirk, 28 July 2011
22. E-mail to John Kirk, 22 Aug. 2011

67

Canadian Coast Guard Auxiliary Unit 59 was practicing retrieval of floating bodies from the sea with its vinyl dummy 'Bob Manikin.' 'Bob' was in the ocean when navigator Bob Thorburn noticed something strange and alerted other crew members. They saw an unusual looking creature about 1,000 feet away. Its head and neck stood well above water. Its long body, dark on one side and lighter on the other, appeared to be resting on the water surface. "Originally we thought it might be a whale, a stellar [sic–meaning a Steller sealion] and then seals," Thorburn said. "What caught my attention was the length (over 20 feet)." Then the animal submerged, apparently straight down, without a splash, and a large circle formed in the water. "There was no trace of 'Bob'," Thorburn said. "We watched for quite a while," he continued. "In the circle, all these bubbles emerged. I've never seen anything like it before." Fortunately, 'Bob' was later found on a nearby beach, not much worse for wear.[23]

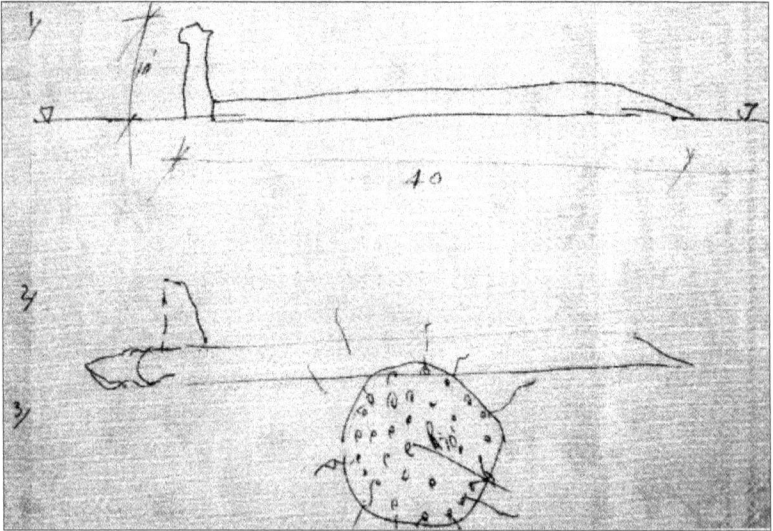

Caddy as seen by the Canadian Coast Guard Auxiliary, near Denman Island, as sketched by Bob Thorburn: 1) first view; 2) after it turned on its side and he saw "a 'chest' fin typical of what's found at the base of Caddy's neck;" 3) the circle formation showing the bubbles surfacing after it dove. *Oceanside Star,* 12 Jan. 2012. (Photo: Authors' file).

---

23. *Oceanside Star,* 12 Jan. 2012

Still further north, Fisherman Allen Chikite saw Caddy near Baker's Pass, between Cortez and Redondo Islands in 1987; "…he drove the boat past what he thought was a large tree sticking out of the water till it started moving and turning it's head… the creature had a giraffe-like head (with small horns) protruding about 6 feet out of the water with a long body (humps) trailing behind… as it swam quickly by the boat he noted the muscles moving on the body that had a similar colour to a Arbutus tree. The sighting lasted a few minutes till it disappeared from sight."[24]

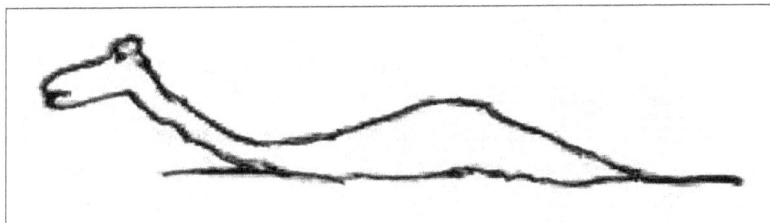

Allan Chikite's Caddy sketch. (Photo: Authors' file)

Not too far away, Marie Hutchinson and her husband, Harold Aune, were cruising in Knight Inlet, one of the deep fjords that indent the coast, in the summer of 2000. They saw what at first looked like a large deadhead. "But through the binoculars," wrote Ms Hutchinson, "I saw sticking up about three feet from the surface of the water a creature unlike anything I had ever come across…The creature was looking in our direction with two huge glistening black eyes… down near the water was a thin line of a mouth running much of the way across the two-foot width of the thing." A longer look revealed that the eyes were probably nostrils. Her husband at first thought they had seen a bull elephant-seal, but later, upon looking up images of elephant seals, agreed that what they had seen was much larger and didn't look like one.[25] That same summer, Tim and Laurice Mock also saw 2 sets of humps, four per set, and a snake-like head in nearby Homfray Channel, part of Toba Inlet.[26]

Tugboat operators travel at a leisurely pace and have plenty of time to observe their surroundings. On September 2, 1995, skipper

24. Report to Jason Walton, 27 Jan. 2007
25. Letter to Paul LeBlond, 19 Jan. 2001
26. *Victoria Times Colonist,* 9 Aug. 1997

Roy Kristmanson and his crew were heading north towards Prince Rupert on board one of Rivtow Marine's tugboats. They had just steamed by the north end of Gil Island (onto which the Queen of the North ran aground in March 2006) passing by the mouth of Douglas Channel. The weather was fine, the sea calm, the visibility excellent. From at least a mile away, Roy spotted a floating object which he could not identify; it seemed to be moving in a nearly rythmic motion. As he approached it, he kept it in sight in his binoculars until the tug was even with it, about 150 feet away. It was then that he realized he was looking at an animal...which was looking back at him. "As long as I live," said Kristmanson, "I'll never forget those eyes. They were large and dark, close set above the snout, in a head that was about three feet long and nearly a foot wide. I was so surprised that I jumped back and hit the radar behind me." He called the attention of his deck hand, Lee Fotz, to the creature and turned the tug towards the animal, which promptly sank below the surface.

At first, the animal had its head sticking out of the water at an angle and was opening and closing its jaws. When the tug came nearest, it put its head down with its jaw at the water surface. That's when Kristmanson realized what he was looking at. He saw neither ears nor teeth. "I was looking straight down its throat through my binoculars and certainly didn't see any teeth." There was movement in the water about 40 feet from the head, which he took to be the animal's tail. No other part of the body was visible. "He looked just like Dino (Fred Flinstone's pet dinosaur)" said Kristmanson.[27]

Caddy was also seen on the west coast of Vancouver Island, near Tofino, BC. In August 1999, Jim Maher and his girlfriend were camping on Indian Island. Maher got up at dawn and was scanning the waters with his binoculars when he spotted "a long thin dark-greyish object protruding about three feet from the water." He wrote, "I saw a strange reptilian head at the top about a foot in length, with two eyes, one on either side, like any reptile or fish. Behind it in the water could occasionally be seen what seemed like bumps or humps where the body obviously continued below the surface. I was shocked to say the least." He went to wake up his girl-

---

27. Interviewed by Paul LeBlond, 12, May 1999

Caddy seen by Jim Maher near Tofino, 1999. (Photo: Authors' file)

friend, who also saw it. Strangely, the animal was reported to have stood still for about 5 minutes before disappearing in the water.[28]

Even more recently, in August 2013, Caddy was seen by Aiden Girard in Cadboro Bay, sporting a large serpentine body, "the size of a small car, head like a seal, or a horse."[29] Later that year in December, it was also seen off Galiano Island by Sylvie Beauregard, a self-professed skeptic ("I always believed that people who claimed to have seen the Loch Ness monster or the Ogopogo were delusional"). She stated that it had a 4-foot long glossy black neck, and a 40-50 foot long body.[30]

Caddy is well and alive in the northeast Pacific coastal waters. It continues to show up in its many forms from California to Alaska, ever surprising and unpredictable. As we shall see, similar creatures also pop up in the fresh water environment, in many rivers and lakes.

---

28. Report to Jason Walton, 21 Feb. 2007
29. Report to Jason Walton, Dec. 2013
30. Report to Paul LeBlond, Dec. 2013

Chapter 7

The Freshwater Cryptids of British Columbia

The province of British Columbia is replete with freshwater cryptids. Most live in lakes while a few have been seen in assorted rivers across the province. Perhaps it would be best to start with the creatures that would also have access to the sea as they may have a bearing on the identity of Cadborosaurus.

On the southwest side of Vancouver Island is Nitinat Lake which drains into the sea through a three kilometer long stretch of water known as Nitinat Narrows. This lake is actually a saltwater fjord some 14 miles long and 3/4 mile wide. It is considered to be one of the top ten windsurfing sites in the world. It is also the home of two cryptids.

The first Nitinat cryptid was reported to John Kirk by Barrie Alden former president of the BC Wildlife Federation.[1] Alden was friendly with the local First Nations people and was told by an elder of the existence of a huge salamander that lived at the lake. Apparently, a crew of native workmen were rebuilding a wooden bridge or boardwalk of some type when they pulled up some planks and unearthed a salamander that was over five feet long. The men fled immediately and refused to return to the site.

The largest known salamander in BC., the Coastal Giant Salamander, *Dicamptodon tenebrosus,* is a mere twelve inches long and therefore an unlikely candidate for that animal. The Japanese and Chinese giant salamander *Megalobatrachus japonicas* grows up to five feet, but is not native to British Columbia.[2]

The second type of cryptid seen in Nitinat Lake is a serpentine creature resembling Cadborosaurus. Sightings of this elusive cryptid are few and far between and we believe that is because this animal does not actually inhabit the lake.[3] Because there is an entrance to the lake from the sea, it is possible that a wayward individual may have strayed into the lake and then left after a time. As the lake is saltwater, there would be no problem for a seagoing sea-serpent to easily adapt to the lake environment.

---

1. Alden, pers. comm. 1992
2. http://www.carcnet.ca/
3. Alden, pers. comm. 1992

A similar occurrence of an oceangoing cryptid possibly entering a lake is that of the creature seen by Clayton Mack, a Nuxalk hunting guide, and Bob Mackie, an American guiding apprentice, who were involved in one of the most bizarre episodes in aquatic cryptid history recorded in a collection of stories about Mack's colourful life known as *Grizzlies and White Guys*.[4]

Mack and Bob Mackie were passing between Second and Third Narrows on Owikeno Lake (connected to Rivers Inlet, in the central British Columbia coast) after doing preparatory work on closing a hunting cabin for the season. Mack saw an animal he thought was a seal and told Mackie to pick up his 0.338 automatic rifle and be ready to shoot the seal, as seals had been wreaking havoc on the coho salmon population in the lake.

As they approached the object it became obvious to Mack and Mackie that this was no seal. The skinny neck was over five feet long and leant forward at an angle as it swam. The head of the creature was small, but it had huge eyes—a featured often described by witnesses who have seen Cadborosaurus—and its coloration was dark, possibly black. Mack insisted that the creature had some kind of shoulder structure that he could see was connected to the neck.

The two men closed in on the creature and Mack gave Mackie the order to fire. The gun went off and Mack was convinced that a crack shot like Mackie—who had shot a grizzly earlier that same day— couldn't possibly miss. The head of the animal darted downward and dived under the water. Mack and Mackie sped to the spot looking for telltale signs of the blood and fat that would float on the surface if a seal had been shot, but there was no trace of either.

Mack peered down under the surface and was stunned to see a huge black object directly beneath their skiff. The object was larger than a grizzly bear, and Mack knew it was time to hightail it out of there when the creature kicked out and made the water boil around the boat. Mack opened the engine and the two hunters took off like there was no tomorrow.

Mackie was adamant that they should not stop until they got to their campsite and insisted that Mack drive the boat up on the beach —just in case the creature followed them—so that they could avoid having to be in the water. This is precisely what Mack did and there was no further sign of the mystery lake creature.

---

4. C. Mack, 1996

After packing and making sure that the cabin at the campsite was prepared for winter, Mack asked Mackie what they had seen. Mackie's response is staggering: he stated that he believed it was a dinosaur and the type that fed on vegetation on trees. Such vegetarian sauropods are supposed to have died off some 65 million years ago.

It is hard to conceive of a sauropod dinosaur living in a fairly cold northern lake. These animals lived in warm tropical climes and the chance of a cold-blooded reptile adapting to frigid waters is next to zero. A more plausible explanation is that Mack and Mackie saw a Cadborosaurus which had entered the lake and was in the Narrows between the lake proper and the sea when it was encountered. Mack kept the story to himself, but on one occasion he spoke to a fellow native who told Mack that his relation David Bernard from Rivers Inlet had seen the same creature many years ago. Mack related that natives he had spoken to would avoid the Narrows after dark as there was something there that had previously spooked them.

Another avenue for movement from the ocean to freshwater is the Fraser River and particularly one of its tributaries, the Harrison River. Some reports of such a freshwater Cadborosaurus are quite controversial. For example, a 1930's newspaper story carried a tale about a bejeweled serpent hundreds of feet long having been sighted in the Harrison River, a story so farfetched that is not even worth considering.[5] However, there is a particularly vivid account by Hans Oluk of an animal seen in nearby Harrison Lake that is worth recounting.

Oluk and a crew onboard the tug *Rivtow Straits* were motoring on Harrison Lake in 1908 when captain Jack Brooks called out to Oluk—who was below deck—to come up and take a look at something. Brooks and Oluk saw the 12–15 foot high head and neck of an unknown creature in the water. It was like no animal the men had ever seen. Brooks was so obviously alarmed by the spectacle of the lake cryptid that he ordered Oluk to go below decks and retrieve his rifle in case the boat was attacked. Oluk recalls he went to

---

5. The Chilliwack Progress (26 Aug. 1936) reported on the "granddaddy of all Ogopogos" seen two days earlier in the Harrison River: three 100 foot long sections that joined together.

retrieve the weapon and by the time he came back to the top the creature was gone.[6]

A First Nations woman named Annie Jim was interviewed by the late Jim Clark—former secretary of the British Columbia Scientific Cryptozoology Club (BCSCC)—who saw the same type of creature in the same lake (Harrison Lake). She advised Clark that the locals named the creature Chunucklas and it was well-known. The last purported sighting of the creature was in 1978 when two women again saw a long-necked creature in the water as they were driving along the eastern shore of the lake.[7]

British Columbia's most publicized lake cryptid is the famous Ogopogo, the denizen of Okanagan Lake and Skaha Lake.[8] Some have posited that Ogopogo and Cadborosaurus are one and the same type of animal because prior to 1926 Okanagan Lake had unfettered access to the Pacific Ocean via the Okanagan River in Canada, and the Okanogan and Columbia Rivers in the United States. The theory here is that an ocean-going animal such as Cadborosaurus navigated the rivers before ultimately settling in Okanagan and Skaha lakes which are connected by a river and a channel.

In 1926 the Columbia, Okanogan and Okanagan Rivers became part of a water system that saw the construction of a series of dams which made it difficult if not impossible for a large creature to move between these rivers and the sea. The thinking is this meant that Ogopogos became landlocked and were no longer able to return to the sea. While the upstream movement theory is plausible and creatures could have moved between Okanagan Lake and the sea, as salmon used to (and still reach Osoyoos Lake today), the idea that Ogopogo and Cadborosaurus are the same type of animal breaks down when the finer details of eyewitness reports from Okanagan Lake are considered.

The two creatures share certain features such as elongated serpentine bodies which—depending on whether they are locomoting or not—are said to show multiple humps, a single large hump or back, coils, loops or, when still, they resemble a log floating on the water. The heads of Caddy and Ogopogo have variously been described as horse, sheep, goat, camel or reptile-like. Ogopogos

---

6. Jim Clark, Pers. Comm. 1989
7. Jim Clark, Pers. Comm. 1989
8. Gaal, A., 1986; Kirk, J, 1998

possess very smooth skin which has been described as whale-like or fish-like. It is very difficult to tell what the texture of the skin of the Naden Harbour carcass, which has been taken as the type specimen of Cadborosaurus,[9] might have been, but eye-witnesses in some sightings report rough skin, coconut-like fibre, scales as well as smooth bodies.

If we take the Naden Harbour carcass as the archetype for Cadborosaurus we will note that this is a camel-headed creature with two ventral flippers and a tail flipper structure as well. Its general appearance shows that creature is serpentine in aspect and that it bears something of a superficial resemblance to Ogopogo. There have been sightings of various other creatures in BC coastal waters that have been designated as Caddy sightings, but we will use the Naden Harbour carcass because there is no doubt whatsoever that it existed, and this allows us to use what we believe was a real unclassified animal as the focal point of our discussion.

To make our comparison between Ogopogo and Cadborosaurus we will use the creatures' appearances out of the water as a gauge. The Naden Harbour carcass was photographed twice by G.V. Boorman and once by F. S. Huband as the carcass lay on an improvised table made of crates. The features described above are obvious to the eye and little further comment is needed (see below, Chapter 8).

Now let us contrast the Naden carcass with descriptions of Ogopogo out of the water supplied by several different witnesses at separate times. The earliest documented sighting of an appearance of Ogopogo out of the water is from 1948. There had been major flooding in Kelowna that year and as John Greig cycled home one night near Mission Creek he heard a hissing sound from the marshy area. As Greig turned around to see what was causing the noise, he encountered a large reptilian creature WALKING in the marsh. Greig knew instantly that this was an Ogopogo and saw enough of it—before it marched back into the lake—to describe its webbed feet.[10]

From the Naden Harbour photos one can deduce instantaneously that the Cadborosaurus specimen does not have legs or feet. It has

---

9. Bousfield and LeBlond, 1995
10. A. Gaal, op. cit. p. 113

flippers. The flippers do not appear to have the weight-bearing capacity to allow a Cadborosaurus to walk comfortably as their flippers seem rather flimsy in comparison to the more substantial flippers of sea lions and certain seals. What distinguishes Ogopogo as a possible separate species or animal is the fact that witnesses have clearly described the legs and feet the animal possesses. Granted the legs and feet aren't very large, but it is clear that Ogopogo does not possess flippers as the Naden Harbour carcass does.

Witness Inez Cooper reported an encounter with Ogopogo in 1976 and shortly after found unidentifiable footprints five inches long and five inches wide on the foreshore where the sighting occurred. They did not match those of any known animal and may indeed have been left by Ogopogo.[11] In 1977 Lilian Vogelgesang and her daughter Jamie-Lea saw Ogopogo in the shallows of Sarson's Beach in Kelowna and Jamie-Lea excitedly pointed out to her mother that Ogopogo was churning up the water with its feet.[12]

Frank, Jim and Orry Reiger had a most amazing experience in 1979 when they watched Ogopogo for no less than 40 minutes as it swam alongside their boat while it appeared to be feeding on kokanee (the fish that is, a landlocked salmon, not the beer of the same name!). They noted that the creature had four legs and used the two rear ones to propel itself through the water.[13]

Since Okanagan Lake has been cut off from the sea since only 1926 it is impossible for a Cadborosaurus of the Naden Harbour variety to have evolved legs of the type seen in Ogopogo specimens in such a short time. It is clear that hard as it may seem to some observers and theoreticians, Ogopogo and Cadborosaurus are not the same type of animal.

There is a possible seagoing relative of Ogopogo in the form of a creature seen by Terry Osland on a beach at Ardmore Point, Saanich Inlet in 1991. (described above, in Chapter 5). Osland was walking her dog along some cliffs when she suddenly saw the face of an unknown animal looking at her from over the cliff edge. It suddenly disappeared and Osland then heard a splash. She peered over the edge of the cliff and could see the creature which was sub-

---

11. Andrew Bennett, pers. comm.
12. A. Gaal, op. cit. p. 118
13. A. Gaal, op. cit. p. 119

stantially larger than a killer whale now in the water. She was able to see its lizard-like tail and the presence of two small feet next to the tail.

The description by Osland of the creature she viewed differs somewhat in appearance to that of the Naden Harbour animal and must be viewed as a different type of animal. However it does bear a cursory resemblance to Ogopogo, but there really is not enough from her description to definitively link it to Ogopogo.

Supporters of the Ogopogo-Cadborosaurus-same-creatures theory are not going to be happy with what we are proposing here. They will invariably ask how it is possible that there could be two different aquatic cryptids in BC. We would simply argue that conclusions ought to be based on observation rather than on theory and that there is so much variety in the descriptions that it is impossible to conclude, even for marine cryptids, that there is a single type of creature.

While Caddy descriptions are really varied, it is not so with BC Lake cryptids. Pretty much all of the descriptions are similar with slight variations in the descriptions of the heads, which can look like sheep, horses, camels and goats. These differences are explainable if one considers that there may be young with sheep or goat-like heads and more mature ones with a stronger profile like a camel or horse. There may also be differences according to the genders of the Ogopogos sighted by observers.

All in all there are 43 lakes and rivers in BC where these unknown lake animals have been seen.[14] One or two may be ascribed to myth and legend and perhaps a couple of others to sightings of sturgeons, but by and large the descriptions are pretty much the same for the denizens of these lakes. One exception is the Cameron Lake creature which deviates in colour—at least in the two photos we have from the lake—as it appears to be whitish or silvery in colour.

The Cameron Lake creature has been the subject of numerous reports in the Canadian press in the past few years.[15] Cameron Lake is connected to the sea through the Qualicum River and one might speculate that a Caddy could have swum from the sea to the lake,

---

14. J. Kirk, 1998

15. e.g., *Nanaimo Daily News*, Sept. 10, 2009; *Globe & Mail,* Sept. 15, 2010; Vancouver *Sun,* Sept. 17, 2010

Cameron Lake cryptid photographed by Brigette Horvath in 2007. She estimates it was about ten feet long. (Photo: Copyright John Kirk and BCSCC, 2010).

and that these two cryptids might be related. However, a major obstacle to that theory is the presence of Little Qualicum Falls between the lake and the river, which the creature would have to negotiate. Anyone who has been to the falls will know that it is an impossibility to swim up these falls and the only other access upwards toward Cameron Lake would be over the precipitous rocks on either side—a feat so difficult for humans with limbs let alone for a flippered cryptid.

To complicate things even further, in addition to aquatic cryptids like Ogopogo and Caddy, there are the giant salamanders mentioned earlier in this section, which are not restricted to just Nitinat Lake. They have been sighted in Cultus Lake (Chilliwack) and Pitt Lake (Pitt Meadows area), as well as in the Fraser River. Some would say it is just too much that there could be three distinct

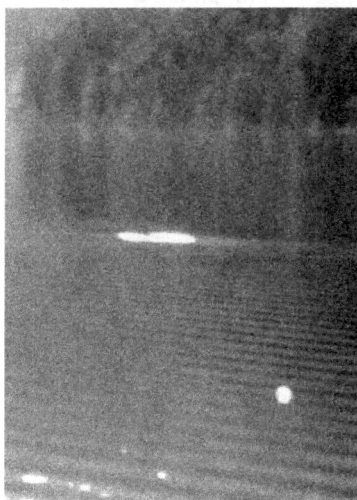

The Cameron Lake cryptid as photographed by Anastasia Broda, May 17, 2012 – 4 to 5 feet long (Photo: Copyright John Kirk and the BCSCC, 2012)

aquatic cryptids in BC, but the facts speak for themselves and it simply is what it is. They are there and need to be studied.

There is the possibility that the eventual discovery of one of the three types of aquatic creatures we have discussed could aid in understanding the other two types, but it probably isn't going to be the case. We are talking about two very different freshwater and one even more different saltwater cryptids which may well have very distinct niches in their respective environments. While we do know that Cadborosaurus and Ogopogo creatures have been seen chasing fish and eating birds, we know absolutely zero about the sustenance required by the salamander-like animals.

It is quite apparent that BC's lake cryptids are an enigma unto themselves and should not be lumped in with the equally perplexing Cadborosaurus question. Perhaps in due time, both these and the giant salamander questions might be answered, but with precious little funding available to mount projects to find these animals, the possibility of solving the mystery remains a long way off.

COLOUR PLATES

This artistic depiction of Cadborosaurus (nicknamed "Caddy") was created by David Peters in 1993, inspired by a 1984 sighting by Jim Thompson, near Vancouver, BC. Sightings of the elusive creature date back to before record-ed history. Its name is derived from modern sightings in Cadboro Bay, which is on the south coast of Vancouver Island (near Victoria) BC. Although there is overwhelming eyewitness evidence that such creatures do indeed inhabit the vast oceans of the world, scientific recognition still awaits the availability of a specimen.(Photo: Copyright: P. LeBlond)

The most noted lake monster is "Nessie," or the Loch Ness Monster, in Scotland. The model seen here sits on a pond behind the Loch Ness Center and Exhibition in Drumnadrochit, Scotland. It is believed to show what people say they have spotted for hundreds of years. This cryptid has become a study unto itself and there is some evidence as to its reality. Loch Ness does have access to the sea and perhaps that is where Nessie originally came from, but eventually became locked in the lake. However, unless the animal lives for hundreds of years, there would have to be a breeding population in the lake. No bones have been found to date so the mystery continues. (Photo: Stara Blazkova at the Czech language Wikipedia—Creative Commons provision.)

Portrait of Caddy: This detail from a remarkable painting by Susan Laurie-Bourque (full painting used for the covers of book by LeBlond and Bousfield, 1995) reflects closely what the Naden Harbour juvenile Caddy might have looked like as an adult. Also, we see here what many witnesses report—a head resembling that of a horse, or even a camel (even to the extent of the stubby horns). Susan's colouring is also very appropriate. We can imagine that an animal such as Caddy might have the colour of sea-weeds or kelp to be as inconspicuous as possible. We can speculate that Caddy's primary enemy of the deep would be whales—both sperm whales (the Naden specimen was found in the stomach of a sperm whale) and killer whales (Orca), and probably sharks. (Photo: Susan Laurie-Bourque)

Stone carvings of unusual sea creatures found in an old monastery near Lough Corrib in western Ireland.

What appears to be a stylized anchor is seen in the top image, indicating a con-nection with the sea.

The carving on the left has a Caddy-like head, and we can see a large fin on its back.

Of course, people in the middle ages were somewhat obsessed with sea monsters and depicted them in their artwork —especially on old maps where they imply mystery and danger in the vast unexplored oceans. Many, if not most, sightings were of animals now known to science, however, some depictions definitely leave us to wonder.(Photos: P. Byrne)

The sea-goddess Thetis, one of the Nereids and the mother of Achilles, the hero of the Trojan War, riding a hippocamp, a classical mythical creature suggested as a cultural model for Caddy. (See page 115). (Photo: Public domain)

The plesiosaur, a large (17–50-foot) Jurassic marine reptile similar to Caddy in its general shape, especially its long neck. That superficial resemblance has been drawn upon to infer that Caddy might be a relic plesiosaur, surviving to this day in the depths of the North Pacific ocean. Plesiosaur experts reject that hypothesis for specific morpho-logical reasons, especially regarding the mode of locomotion and flexure of the body. (Photo: Wikipedia—Creative Commons provision)

A Pacific Coast plesiosaur: the skeleton of an elasmosaur found in 1988 in the Puntledge River area, Courtenay, BC, the first one of its kind found west of the Rockies. This animal was a fierce predator, over 65 feet long and fed on fish and smaller marine reptiles. It would have been in competition and perhaps sometimes prey to giant mosasaurs, another family of marine reptiles. (Photo: Courtenay Museum and Paleontology Centre)

British Columbia's coast. There are thousands of islands and countless bays and coves. It is perhaps these features that resulted in Caddy essentially selecting this region as "home."

(Photo: Image from Google Earth; Image Landsat; Image IBCAO; Data SIO, NOAA, US Navy NGA GEBCO)

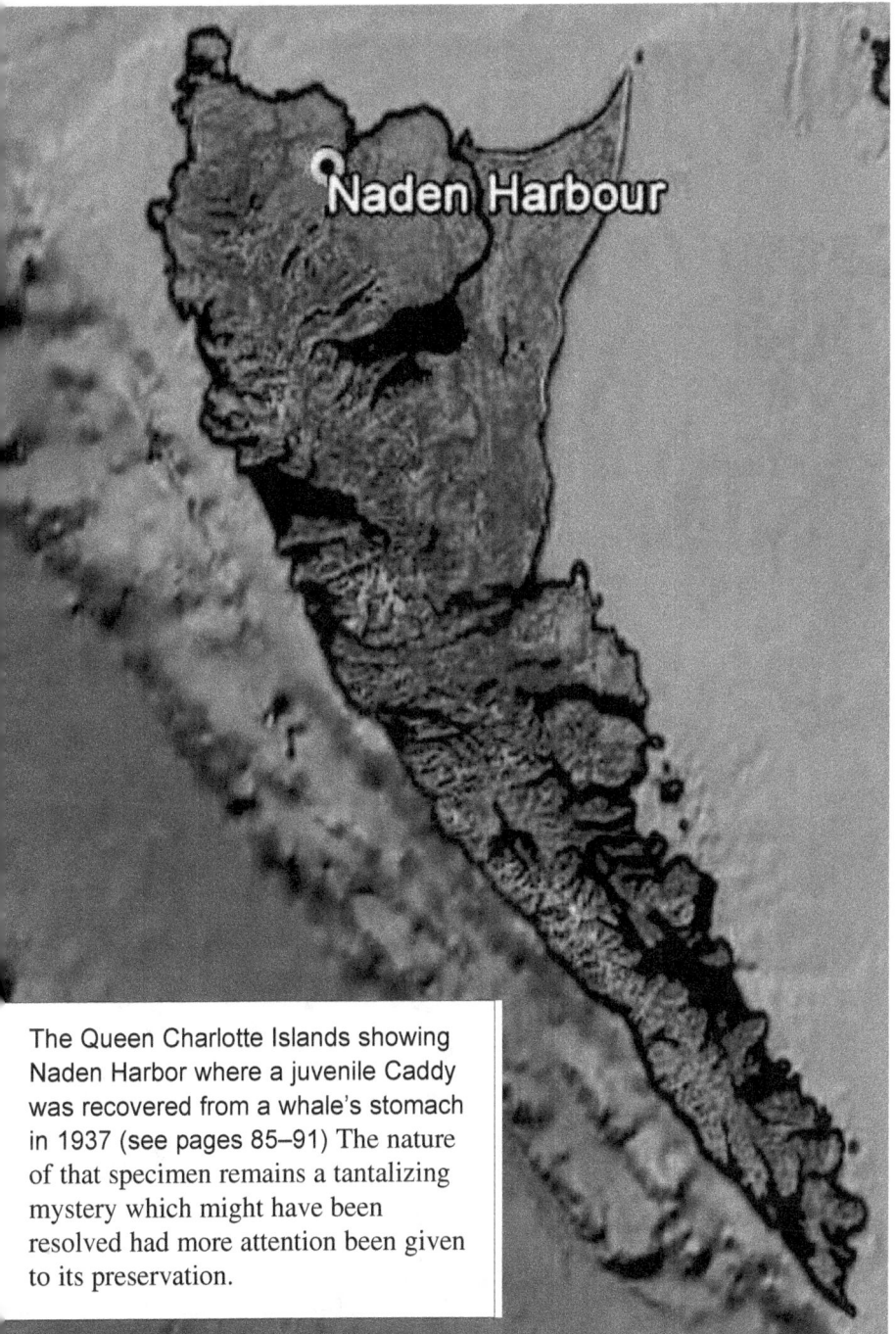

The Queen Charlotte Islands showing Naden Harbor where a juvenile Caddy was recovered from a whale's stomach in 1937 (see pages 85–91) The nature of that specimen remains a tantalizing mystery which might have been resolved had more attention been given to its preservation.

(Photo: Image from Google Earth; Image Landsat; Image IBCAO; Data SIO, NOAA, US Navy NGA GEBCO)

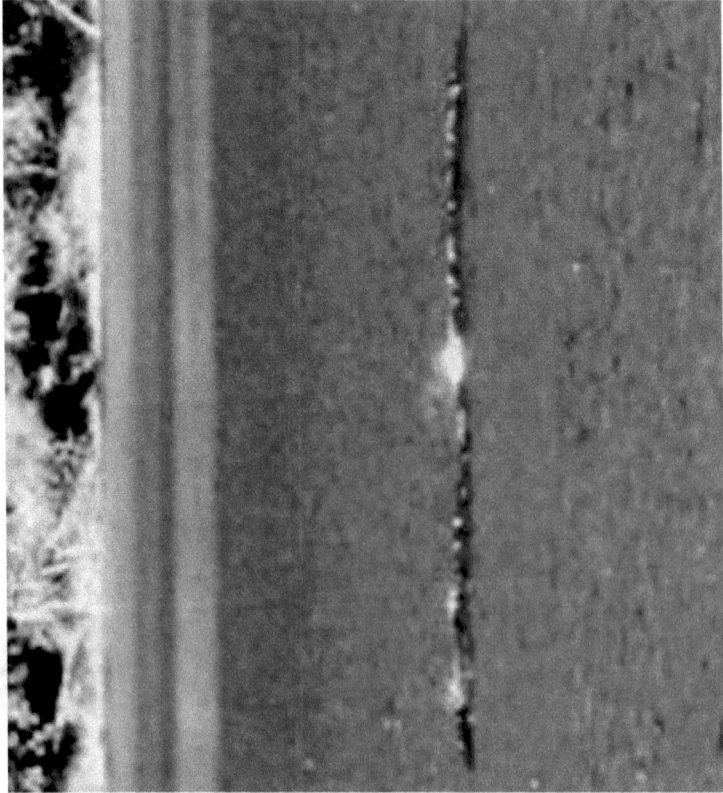

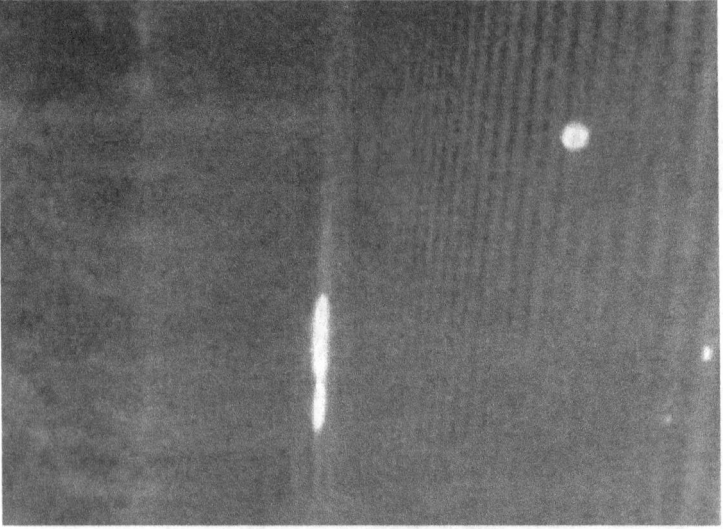

Left: Two unidentified animals in Cameron Lake, BC as photographed by Brigette Horvath on July 30, 2007. A third animal was also reported on the scene observing the other two. Right: Unknown animal seen on the surface of Cameron Lake, BC by Anastasia Broda, May, 2012. She also took several other photos of the animal which appears to be about 6 feet long. (Photos: Copyright 2012, 2007, John Kirk and the British Columbia Scientific Cryptozoology Club)

A group of fishermen and an Alaska Fish and Game employee (third from the left) looking at a beached carcass at Homer, Alaska, of what appears to be an unusual sea creature. The size would likely indicated that it was a juvenile, however, indications are that it was a decayed lemon shark. Whatever the animal was, we can surmise that finding a carcass of this nature will be the best way to prove Caddy is a living species. All we need is a small sample and DNA analysis will tell the full story. (Photo: Trevor Johnson)

MUSÉE DU FJORD

Monstres

MARINS

LES ÉDITIONS GID

Cover of the catalog of a exhibit on sea monsters at the Musée du Fjord, a museum located at La Baie, Quebec.(http://www.monstresmarins.ca/). Here we see the tradi-tional age-old concept of terrifying sea monsters attacking ships and eating sailors. There is little to support such notions in general, and nothing with regard to Caddy. If anything, Caddy is shy and reclusive, thus making it very difficult to get good pho-tographs of the animal. Modern-day motorized pleasure craft are quite large, and always noisy, Caddy would hear them long before the animal could be sighted. A sail boat would likely be best for "Caddy seeking." (Photo: Musee du Fjord)

L'ILLUSTRÉ
DU PETIT JOURNAL
DIMANCHE GRAND HEBDOMADAIRE POUR TOUS 50
11 MARS 1934

UN MONSTRE MARIN INCONNU

A magazine cover showing an artistic rendering of the Querqueville carcass found on a beach in Normandy in 1934. Neither the artist nor the onlookers recognized the decayed and deformed carcass— later identified as that of a basking shark—and mistook it for an unknown sea monster. (Photo: *L' Illustré* magazine)

Is this Caddy swimming near the beach? A still photo of these rocks could be mistaken for an animal...a misinterpretation unlikely to happen in a video. (Photo: Authors' file)

A sketch of the sea-serpent seen from H.M.S *Daedalus* in the South Atlantic in 1848. Captain Peter M'Quhae described it as "at least 60 feet long." The animal came "so close to the ship," he added, "that had it been a man of my acquaintance, I should easily have recognized his features with the naked eye." (Photo: Public domain)

In 1990 Canada Post featured what they call "Ogopogo" on a postage stamp in their Canadian Folklore – Legendary Creatures series. Although the artistry is wonderful, the depiction is totally incorrect for Ogopogo. The stamp designer tells us that while the animals is shown as "Ogopogo" he incorporated features to make the image more or less generic to represent all of Canada's unrecognized lake creatures. Nevertheless, little (if anything) is similar to what we know of all such animals.

As to Ogopogo, this animal is likely the same, or very close in appearance to Caddy. Although we cannot say they are directly related, the possibility exists.

Whatever the case, the depiction on of a Canadian water cryptid on a postage stamp does serve to show that sightings of such are deeply embedded in Canadian history. (Photo: © Canada Post, 1990)

Chapter 8

Pics and Bones

Hundreds of encounters at sea and glimpses from shore of these strange creatures soon convinced the public of the presence of large animals unknown to science. That was however not enough for the Vancouver Tourist Association, who wanted pictures to back up visual reports, and certainly not enough for professional zoologists, who needed a specimen to examine and identify. It is not surprising that the discovery of large carcasses stranded on beaches attracted attention as potential evidence which could satisfy the skeptics.

In 1934, soon after Caddy's public appearance in the Victoria newspapers, the badly decomposed remains of a 30 foot long creature were found by fisherman Hugo Sandstrom on Henry Island, off the north end of Porcher Island, near Prince Rupert, BC. Dr. Neal Carter, then director of the Dominion Fisheries Experimental Station in Prince Rupert, went to investigate in the fisheries patrol boat and found the remains lying on the beach, just below the high-water mark. "The creature was possibly thirty feet long when alive," wrote Carter. "Some of the tail appears to be missing. I believe it had been there for some six weeks or two months because of the advanced state of decomposition. The skin resembled sandpaper, rougher than that of dogfish, or shark. The upper part of the body was covered with hair, the lower part with spines." Carter found no bones in the creature's body except for the backbone: no ribs nor any other bones. Flesh still clinging to the backbone was red, similar to beef in appearance, which, to Carter, "put the creature out of the fish class." There was some evidence for fins, or flipper-like projections of cartilaginous material, about four feet long; the head was also described as cartilaginous and "like that of a calf."[1]

The carcass was soon heralded as "possible proof of the existence of Caddy." The *New York Herald Tribune* featured a front-page headline: "Remains of Hairy Sea-Serpent Silence Skeptics,

---

1. *Vancouver Province,* 22 Nov. 1934, p. 1

Baffle Scientists." linking the carcass directly to "Hiaschuckaluck cadborosaurus."[2] Professor Trevor Kincaid, of the University of Washington, thought that the creature was something previously unknown in animal life. "If it was 30 feet long," he said, "it wasn't a sea lion, or a walrus, and if it had hair and quills, it wasn't a whale."[3] The *London Illustrated News* published a picture of the skeleton exhibited on the wharf in Prince Rupert, offering its readers a choice of interpretations with the caption: A Canadian 'Monster': Sea-Cow, Basking Shark or Cadborosaurus?[4] It also showed, on the same page, for comparison, skeletons of a Steller's Sea-Cow and of a Basking Shark. The sea-cow, with its massive rib cage stands in sharp contrast with the giant shark, all back-bone except for its large jaw.

Pieces of the carcass were sent to experts for identification. Francis Kermode, then director of the Provincial Museum in Victoria (now the Royal Museum) said that he had never seen anything like this before and that: "It certainly was not a whale."[5] He ventured the suggestion that the animal might be the last survivor of Steller's sea-cow, thought to have been extinct for well over a century.[6] Other parts were sent to the Pacific Biological Station of the Department of Fisheries, in Nanaimo, to be examined by its director, Dr. W.A. Clemens, British Columbia's senior fisheries biologist. From characteristic features of its skin and bones, Clemens recognized the carcass as definitely belonging to a basking shark.[7] The basking shark, up to 40 feet in length, is a frequent visitor to BC waters. It is often seen at the surface, sluggish as a log and easily approached by boat. Its bones are soft and cartilaginous and decompose rapidly, although the vertebrae are more durable. The scales of its skin are small and sharp, like sandpaper.

2. *New York Herald Tribune,* 23 Nov. 1934, p. 1
3. *Vancouver Sun,* 23 Nov. 1934, p. 9
4. *London Illustrated News,* 15 Dec. 1934, p 19.
5. *New York Times,* 26 Nov. 1934, p. 17
6. *Vancouver Sun,* 26 Nov. 1934, p. 1
7. ibid.

The Henry Island carcass, on the wharf in Prince Rupert (*London Illustrated News,* 1934) (Photo: Public domain)

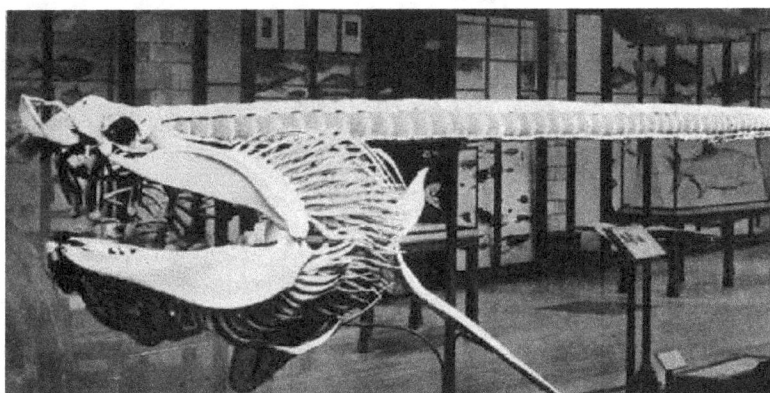
Skeleton of a basking shark (*London Illustrated News,* 1934) (Photo Public domain)

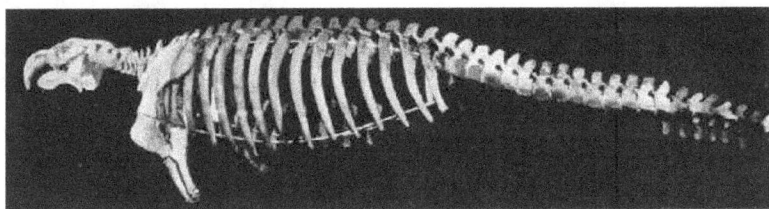
Skeleton of Steller's sea-cow (*London Illustrated News,* 1934) (Photo: Public domain)

This was neither the first nor the last time that decomposing basking sharks were to fool laymen and experts alike. Heuvelmans has presented a number of examples of misidentification of stranded carcasses of basking sharks. When rotting away on the beach, basking sharks lose their softer tissues first, starting with the lower jaws and gill structure, leaving a "long-neck plesiosaur" shape and eventually, as in the Henry Island carcass, only the round vertebrae, easily distinguished from those of the sea-cow. The fibers of the surface muscles break up into whiskers when the skin rots and the flesh is discoloured.[8]

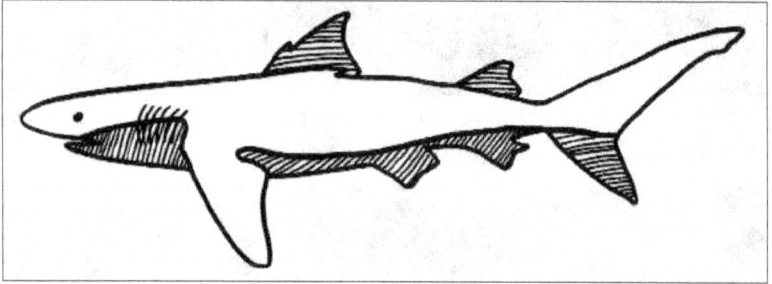

Transformation of a rotting shark into a long-neck creature. (Artwork/Photo: P. LeBlond)

It didn't take very long for a more likely candidate to manifest itself. The most promising of all potential Caddy carcasses was not found stranded on a beach, but in the stomach of a sperm whale.

Long before people learned to love them and wanted to "save" them, whales were quite common in North Pacific waters and were fair prey to bold Native fishermen hunting grey whales, adventurous Yankee whalers, who caught mostly right whales, and eventually, to a small local mechanized industry, equipped to catch the remaining larger and faster whales. Until late in the 19th century, humpbacks could still be seen frolicking in the Salish Sea; giant baleen and toothed whales, blue and sperm, were still common offshore.[9] However, the failure of early attempts at developing a coastal whaling industry, capable of hunting the larger whales, was to be "attributed more to the want of proper appliances than to the scarcity of whales, which are as numerous as ever," concluded the British Columbia Fisheries Commission in 1871.[10] The adoption of mod-

---

8. Heuvelmans, B. 1968, p. 134

9 .Webb, R. L. 1988

10. Report of the British Columbia Fisheries Commission, 1905-07, p. 62

ern whaling methods developed mainly by Svend Foyn in Norway, using fast steam-powered chaser boats and cannon-fired exploding grenade harpoons, soon made it possible to catch and kill the larger whales. Successful and profitable whaling took place over the first half of the twentieth century, based on shore stations on Vancouver Island and the Queen Charlotte Islands. Chaser boats towed their catches to these stations, where they were cut up and rendered for oil. The history of whaling in the north Pacific has been extensively documented by R.L. Webb;[11] William Hagelund, who was a whaler in his youth, has vividly described his adventures during the last years of the coastal whaling industry in his book *Whalers No More*.[12]

In 1937, the Consolidated Whaling Corporation, based in Bellevue, Washington state, operated two whaling stations in the Queen Charlotte Islands, at Rose Harbour on Graham Island, in the south, and at Naden Harbour on Moresby Island. Activity at the Naden Harbour whaling station was concentrated in the summer. The chaser ships (the six 'colour' boats so called because they were all named after a colour) and their crews, as well as the shore teams of flensers, packers and auxiliary personnel, sailed up in the spring and stayed until the weather turned stormy in the fall. The whole operation was under the direction of general superintendant Alphus Dominique Garcin; whenever Mr. Garcin left Naden for Rose, F.S. Huband replaced him as station manager.

In mid-summer 1937, one of the chaser boats brought in a sperm whale, caught off the coast on the same day. Cutting up the carcass, the flensers came upon a strange creature in the whale's stomach, where they were looking for ambergris which, at that time, was worth its weight in gold as a valued product for the perfume industry. The animal was unfamiliar enough for work to stop and for Mr. Huband to be alerted. Hagelund mentions the event;[13] it was also remarkable enough to deserve mention in the Canadian Department of Fisheries Newsletter published in September 1937.[14]

---

11. Webb, R. L., op. cit.
12. Hagelund, W., 1987
13. Hagelund, W, op. cit., p. 177
14. Fisheries News Bulletin, Vol VIII, No. 95, Dept. Fisheries, Ottawa, Sep. 1937, p. 2

James Wakelen was employed at that time at Naden Harbour as a blacksmith. When interviewed by Bousfield and LeBlond at his home in Victoria in 1994, he clearly remembered the event, the excitement caused among the oriental flensers by the unusual creature and how all station personnel came to gawk at it. In a subsequent conversation with Jason Walton, Wakelen insisted that "other than a thin white film covering the body from the whale's stomach, the animal was completely intact..." Walton commented that "lots of animals do look very different after losing body fluids, stages of decomposition..." But, Walton continued, "he cut me off and repeated that this was one intact, complete animal and the queerest thing he had ever seen." There is thus some confidence that the carcass, as it appears in the photographs taken at the time, was not significantly deformed from its ingestion by the whale.

The whale had been harpooned on the fishing grounds off Langara Island, towed to Naden Harbour and flensed soon afterwards. During the short waiting period (10–12 hours, according to Wakelen) some slight digestion of the surface features of the creature may have taken place in the whale's stomach. However, the body was essentially intact and easily distinguishable from any marine animal previously known to the whaling station workers. It was certainly totally unlike any other deep-water prey animals, such as the six-gilled shark, ragfish, or giant squid regularly encountered by the flensers in their search for ambergris in the whales' digestive system.

Mr. Huband decided the creature was so unusual that some record of it should be made, and he had the specimen prepared for photography. The animal was laid out on a five-foot table on the boardwalk, the top surface lengthened by upended packing boxes; the top of the tables and the elevated background frame were draped with white sheets, suitably positioned behind the head, neck and trunk, to enhance contrast. Prints from the original photographic negatives made by Mr. Huband have been preserved. One of them had already appeared in the press;[15] a copy was also found in the B.C. Provincial Archives.[16] Another, taken from a slightly different

15. *Victoria Daily Colonist,* 31 Oct. 1937
16. BC Provincial Archives, catalogue number HP52840; negative No H-4767

angle, was published in Hagelund's *Whalers No More* as a "sea oddity." Captain Hagelund obtained the photo from the Vancouver Maritime Museum, where further research showed it to be part of a folder of 38 photographs attributed to G.V. Boorman, first-aid officer at the Rose and Naden Harbour stations. The last two of these depict the unidentified carcass as: 'The remains of a Sperm Whale's Lunch, a creature of reptilian appearance 10 ft 6 in in length with animal-like vertebrae and a tail similar to that of a horse. The head resembles that of a large dog with features of a horse and the turn down nose of a camel."[17]

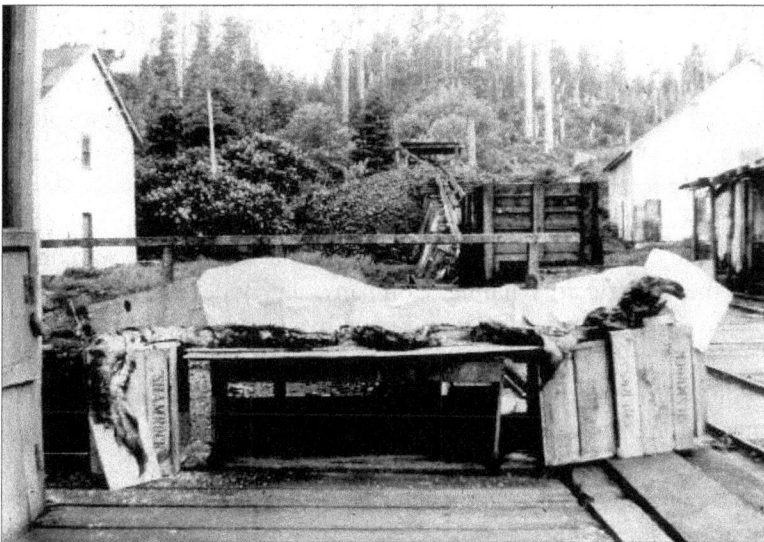

The Naden Harbour specimen. (G. V. Boorman photo, Public domain)

The Fisheries Department Newsletter described it as "about 10 feet long, having a head similar to a large dog's, animal-like vertebrae, and a tail resembling a single blade of gill bone as found in

17. Page 11 of what are probably the original photographer's notes penciled on a pad of 3 inch x 5.5 inch paper stapled to the inside back cover of an album entitled, "Photos by Mr. G. V. Boorman, First-Aid Officer, The Consolidated Whaling Corp.Ltd., Rose Harbour, Queen Charlotte Islands." Vancouver Maritime Museum.

whales' jaws.[18] Another eye-witness, cited by Hagelund, was an old-time whaler, Finn John, who said the specimen "had a horse-like head with large limpid eyes and a tuff of whiskers on each cheek. Its long slender body was covered by a fur-like material, with the exception of its back, where spiked horny plates over-lapped each other. It had skin-covered flippers and a spade-shaped tail like a sperm whale."[19]

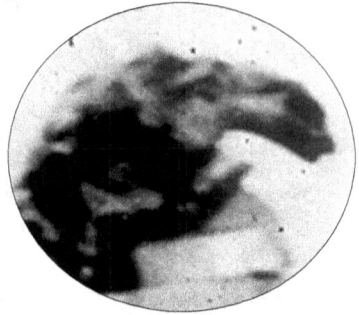

Enlargement of the Naden creature's head as seen in the previous photograph.

Wakelen's recollection, in a phone call with E. Bousfield, in 2007 (Wakelen now deceased, was 94 at the time, with quite good memory) was that "following photography, the carcass was coiled up and preserved in salt." It was then sent by small boat to Masset and thence by CPR boat to Vancouver, a ten day trip. On July 15th, it already had dwelt for a week in a tub of acetone in the warehouse of the American Whaling Company, in Bellevue, Washington, where it apparently was "gazed upon by scores of our local citizenry."[20] Working backwards, the sperm whale, with its "lunch," would have been captured towards the end of June. Attempts at finding, through press and radio, people in the Seattle area who might, as children, have seen the remains of the sea-serpent on display have so far only brought up a person whose grandmother had heard about it at the time.

The Bellevue American announcement goes on to state that the carcass was to be shipped "this week to a Victoria Biological Station" to be examined by experts. On the other hand, Boorman's photo album contains a note to the effect that part of the carcass was shipped to the Nanaimo Biological Station soon after its discovery. There might have been some confusion as to where the specimen was to be sent—perhaps parts of it were sent to each destination.

---

18. Fisheries News Bulletin, loc. cit.

19. Hagelund, op. cit., p. 177

20. *Bellevue American,* Vol VII, No.42, July 15, 1937

THE BELLEVUE AMERICAN
VOL. VII, No. 42.   July 15, 1937

Discover Sea Serpent

To those skeptics who were of the opinion that sea-serpents were the result of too much moonshine whiskey, let it be known that a genuine, in the flesh, sea-serpent has dwelt in a tub of acetone in the warehouse of the American Pacific Whaling company for the past week.

The serpent, witch is alleged to be a mere baby, is ten feet long, has a head similar to that of a horse, and wears considerable long brown hair.

The first two paragraphs of the article announcing the presence of the Naden Harbour carcass to be seen at the whaling company dock in Bellevue, Washington.

Certainly, something was sent to the BC Provincial Museum since its director, Francis Kermode, had a statement to make on July 23, 1937.

MAMMAL NOT CADDY'S SON
Portions of Sea Monster Sent to Museum
Are From Baleen Whale

A theory advanced in Vancouver that portions of a marine mammal taken from the body of a sperm whale might have been part of a young sea serpent which was an offspring of Victoria's famous Cadborosaurus was definitely exploded today by Francis Kermode, director of the provincial museum.

Mr. Kermode said there was little doubt that the portion of a backbone, the piece of baleen and the portion of skin forwarded to the museum were pieces of a baleen whale, which he believes was of premature birth.

The pieces were taken from a sperm whale caught at Naden Harbour in the Queen Charlotte Islands.

The backbone is about six feet long.[21]

Having only part of the specimen to examine, it would have been difficult for Mr Kermode to make a definitive assessment of its nature. While his position as director of the Provincial Museum added authority to his views, one should recall that Kermode was a taxidermist by training and profession, with little background in zoology and might have been confused when faced with an unfamiliar animal. The curator of vertebrate animals at the

For comparison purposes, here is a fetal baleen whale. Holding the carcass are A. Nixon (left) and James Wakelen. James Wakelen Sr., the station accountant is in front. (Photo courtesy of J. Wakelen)

Provincial Museum at that time was Dr. Ian McTaggart-Cowan, fresh from a Ph.D in zoology at the University of California at Berkeley. Unfortunately, he was away on field duties on the date of Kermode's press announcement. When he returned, a few days later, no material was available for viewing, nothing had been preserved: there was no record of the museum ever having received part of the Naden carcass. A account of the early history of the Provincial Museum mentions serious issues with Kermode's record keeping in the late 1930s: "There is so little material, in particular so little correspondence, one researcher has concluded that Kermode must have had a bonfire in the late 30s, leaving in the files only those documents which showed him in a favourable mode."[22]

21. *Vancouver Province,* 23 July 1937
22. Corley-Smith, P., 1989, p. 45

When showed the photographs of the Naden carcass, McTaggart-Cowan readily admitted that the creature didn't look like anything he had ever seen. As to the workers at the whaling station, they could recognize a baleen-whale fetus when they saw one! It's thus rather likely that Kermode misidentified the specimen.

Finally, as there are no remains of the Naden carcass, all that's left are solidly authenticated photos of an unknown creature, which may (or may not) have any relation to Caddy as seen by eye-witnesses. Perhaps, but it was not enough to satisfy even the Vancouver Tourist Association. Nevertheless, the Naden carcass has played an important role as the basis of a scientific description of Caddy,[23] and we shall return to it later.

Another carcass was found in 1941 on Kitsilano Beach, Vancouver, and dubbed "Sarah the Sea Hag" by the press. Again it was touted as possible remains of Caddy. "She had a large horse-like head with flaring nostrils and eye sockets; a tapering snake-like body 12 feet long; and traces of long coarse hair on the skin."[24] Because of the immediate proximity of the University of British Columbia, it was possible for Dr. W.A. Clemens and his junior colleague Dr. Ian McTaggart-Cowan (by then both professors in the university's Zoology Department) to reach the scene quickly and examine the stinking carcass. "We're not sure if it's a basking shark," said Dr. Clemens, "but there is no doubt that it is of the shark family."[25] G.V Boorman, formerly of the Naden Harbour whaling station, had by then become a private in the army and was stationed nearby. On the basis of his examination of the stomach content of 4,000 whales in ten years, he claimed familiarity with sharks in various degrees of decomposition or digestion. "If that's a shark, I'll eat my uniform", said Boorman. "I've seen the skeletons of scores of varieties of sharks and they had no resemblance to these remains." He swore that the "marine monster discovered in the stomach of a sperm whale in 1937 was the twin sister of odoriferous Sarah."[26] It's a statement which significantly muddies the waters and leaves doubt as to the nature of both carcasses. Again, unfortunately, the remains were not preserved.

---

23. Bousfield and LeBlond, 1995
24. *Vancouver Province,* 5 Mar. 1941, p. 15
25. ibid.
26. ibid.

Further strandings didn't bring anything new. The large carcass discovered by Henry Schwarz on Vernon Island, in Barkley Sound, was at first thought to be a ribbon fish, but was soon positively identified by Dr. Clifford Carl, Kermode's successor at the Provincial Museum, as a basking shark.[27] Similarly, the rotting carcass found by Mrs. Ruth Cobert partially buried in a sandy beach on Whidbey Island, Washington, was interpreted by Dr. A. D. Welander, of the University of Washington as yet another basking shark.[28]

An opportunity for obtaining a Caddy carcass as an ocean "road kill" arose in Saanich Inlet in May 1947 when Ernest Lee and Henry Gilbert rammed an apparently wounded Caddy. Lee reported the following:

> I was fishing on Mackenzie Bay, Saanich Inlet, when I saw Caddy. It seemed to be wounded, and swimming in circles, so I ran the boat alongside and had a good look. The head was like a seal, with a neck about 15 feet long, a big fin in the middle of the back and a tail similar in shape to a salmon or a shark. It was about 35 feet in length over all. I think it was some type of a shark. It had a wound on the back of the head, and could not go under the water for more than a few seconds at a time. I went on fishing, and at 8 o'clock picked up Harry Gilbert at Brentwood to see if we could catch it. After trying to hook it with the anchor, without success, we thought we could ram it with the boat. We hit it twice and then it sank and did not rise again
>
> I have considered that perhaps it was a shark, after all, with that big fin.[29]

If a full-size or even a juvenile Caddy was not available, how about a baby one? W. Hagelund described in his memoirs how he captured, and released, an animal which later reminded him of the Naden carcass.[30] Years after his whaling days, he and his family

27. *Vancouver Sun,* 8 Dec.1947
28. Whidbey News Times, 3 Oct. 1963, p. 1
29. *Vancouver Province,* 21 May 1943, p. 13
30. Hagelund, op. cit., p. 178

were yachting through the Gulf Islands; they anchored in Pirate's Cove, DeCourcy Island, near Nanaimo, BC. Hagelund wrote the following:

> With my two sons and their grandfather in our centre-cockpit sloop, we spotted a small surface disturbance in the small anchorage where we had dropped the hook for the night. Lowering the dinghy, my youngest son Gerry and I rowed out to investigate. We found a small eel-like creature swimming along with its head completely out of the water, the undulation of its long slender body causing portions of its spine to break the surface. My first thought that it was a sea-snake was quickly discarded when, on drawing closer, I noticed the dark limpid eyes, large in proportion to the slender head, which had given it a seal-like appearance when viewed from the front. When it turned away, a long, slightly hooked snout could be discovered.

Hagelund and his son brought the animal on board for examination and put it in a large plastic bucket for the night. He went on to describe it as follows:

> It was about 16 inches long and one inch in diameter. His lower jaw had a set of sharp tiny teeth, and his back was protected by plate-like scales, while his underside was covered in a soft yellow fuzz. A pair of small, flipper-like feet protruded from his shoulder area, and a spade-shaped tail proved to be two tiny fins that overlapped each other.

Hagelund was planning to take the strange little animal to the Pacific Biological Station in Nanaimo, but listening to it scratching the sides of the bucket in its efforts to escape, he took pity on it and threw it back overboard. It is only later, when he came across a news clipping of the Naden carcass that he realized the similarities between the two creatures.

Woodley et al [31] have suggested that the animal captured, and then released by Hagelund, was most likely a pipefish (*Syngnathus*

---

31. Woodley et al, 2011

griseolineatus) commonly seen in the Strait of Georgia. Bousfield and LeBlond [32] pointed out that a comparison of the pipefish with a sketch provided by Hagelund shows significant differences: the pipefish has no neck, nearly fused jaws, no posterior paired appendages (pelvic fins), a pronounced dorsal fin, a small vertically oriented tail fin, and plates encircling the whole body (not just on the back and side as in Hagelund's creature). It is not, however, impossible that over the years Hagelund's memory might have transformed a pipefish into the sketch that he drew from memory.

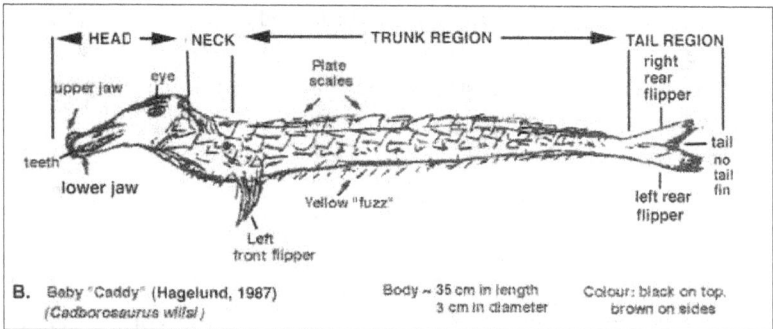

B. Baby "Caddy" (Hagelund, 1987) Body ~ 35 cm in length Colour: black on top,
(*Cadborosaurus willsi*) 3 cm in diameter brown on sides

Hagelund's "baby Caddy" (Photo: Authors' file)

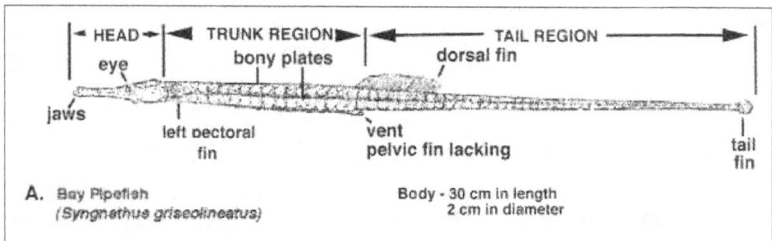

A. Bay Pipefish Body - 30 cm in length
(*Syngnathus griseolineatus*) 2 cm in diameter

The pipefish (*Syngnathus griseolineatus*). (Photo: Authors' file)

The subsequent capture in a crab trap in Ganges Harbour, Saltspring Island, of a specimen very similar to that seen by Hagelund provides some support against the pipefish interpretation. Sam Bowes, the crab fisherman, could not find the likeness of a 3 feet long slender eel-like creature in Hart's Pacific Fishes of Canada,[33] but recognized it instantly in Hagelund's sketch.[34] Unfortunately, the odd creature was chucked over the side after a

---

32. Bousfield and LeBlond, 2011
33. Hart, 1973
34. Letter to E. Bousfield, Feb. 1998

brief examination and one must again rely on witnesses' memory and interpretation. Whether these unusual little animals have anything to do with the Naden carcass and Caddy as described by eyewitnesses remains entirely a matter of conjecture.

Ivan Sanderson was a friend of Bernard Heuvelmans and a pioneer cryptozoologist. Everywhere he went, he gathered information about animals, be they common, rare or cryptids. Two items from his findings may be pertinent to the search for Caddy. The first is an underwater photograph of a "15–20 ft. long sea-serpent" (Marvin, as it was dubbed) which moved close to an underwater camera at a

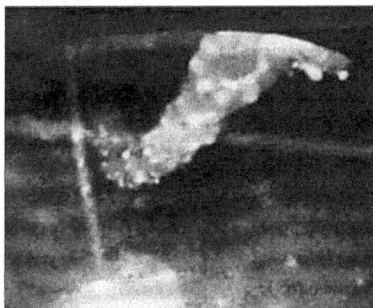

"Marvin," underwater photo from Santa Barbara Channel, 1966. (Photo: Authors' file)

Shell Oil installation in the Santa Barbara Channel in 1966. There's a remarkable similarity between its head and that of the Naden carcass.[35]

Another finding of Sanderson was an echogram obtained by a fishing boat dragging for shrimp in Shelikov Strait, Alaska, which he published in Argosy magazine in 1970 as "concrete proof of the existence of a genuine marine longneck."[36]

Even in the absence of any suspicion of tampering or misinterpretation, a single photo or echogram without further context and control is at best a supporting clue and will not be generally accepted as "concrete

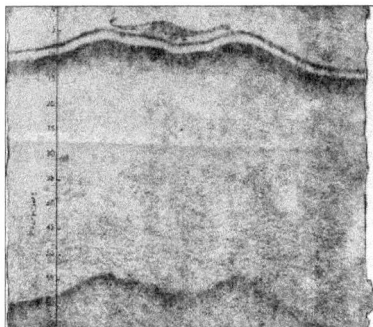

Part of an echogram published by I. Sanderson showing a "longneck" just above the bottom. Depths in fathoms (1 fathom = 6 feet). (Sanderson, 1970). (Photo: Authors' file)

35. http://www.cryptomundo.com/bigfoot-report/marvin-the-monster/
36. I. Sanderson, 1970

proof." We show these images for the sake of interest and completeness and certainly not as proofs of anything.

Of much greater interest and impact is a video of a whole Caddy pod taken by eyewitnesses in Alaskan waters on June 30, 2007. Salmon fishermen Kelly Nash, with his sons Jason and Kyle, were gill-netting in Schooner Channel, Nushagak Bay, an inner arm of Bristol Bay. Having deployed their nets parallel to a long sand bar, they were proceeding to close the upstream (north) end to funnel and trap migrating salmon. They saw, swimming closely together, a pod of large animals swimming first north and then reversing their course when detecting the fishing nets. A plan view of the situation, as sketched by Mr. Nash, shows the position of the fishing vessel *Super Sport,* the deployment of their nets, the location of the sand bar and of the pod of cryptids, approximately 35 yards from the boat. A dispersed group of belugas were also present on the opposite side of the fishing boat.

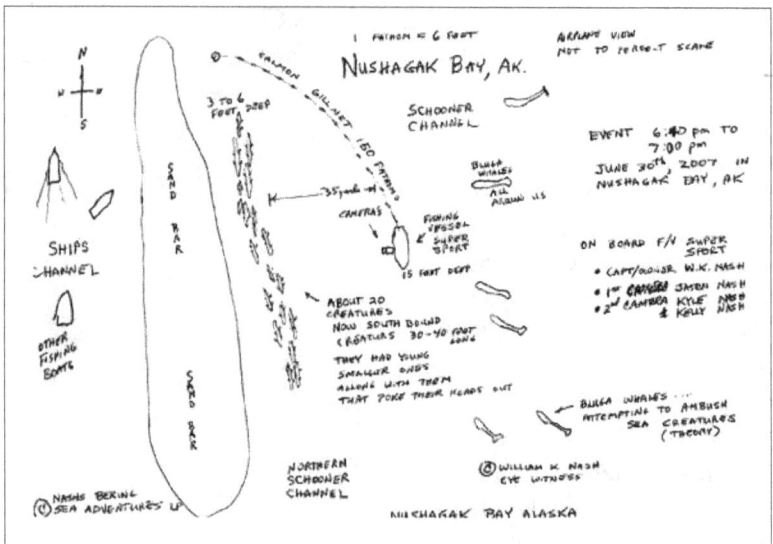

Plan view of cryptid pod sighting in Nushagak Bay; original sketch by Kelly Nash. (Photo: W. K. Nash, used with permission.)

According to Nash, there were about 20 creatures, large and small; the larger ones about 40 ft long. They appeared to have a "long neck (12 feet long, 1.5 feet diameter); small head (like brontosaurus, with bulgy eyes well forward... Boeing 747 look); body about twice-three times as broad as neck, but unlikely to be very big as they were swimming closely together; spikes on back but not on neck; small long ridge/fin on neck, not really a mane."

Nash's movie was taken with a SONY Handycam and subsequently digitally mastered. A group of belugas was also seen "all around us"; Nash thought they might be trying to ambush the cryptids... The weather that day was rainy with moderate winds. Water droplets are seen on the boat's windshield; the horizon on the video bobs up and down with the motion of the boat (hence the need for image stabilization to keep the subject in the middle of the screen).

The film shows the animals swimming to the left. There are clearly many of them, swimming closely to each other. The movement is in the vertical plane. The leading animal is clearly seen to swim first with its head alternately under and above water; another part of its back emerges some distance behind the head and keeps up with it. At one point, it appears that the lead animal blows (from the back of its head?)

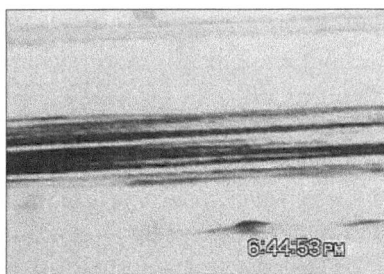

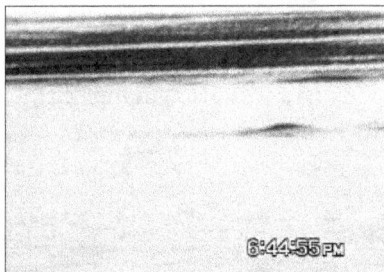

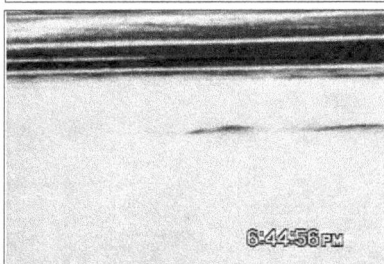

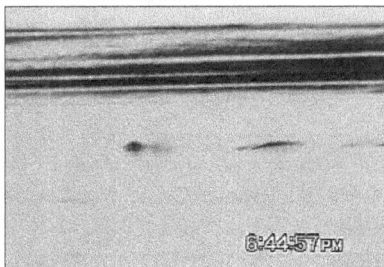

6:44:53 PM

6:44:55 PM

6:44:56 PM

6:44:57 PM

Sequence of four frames of Nash's video, video showing the gradual emergence of the head of one of the animals observed. There is some evidence of blowing behind the head in the last frame. (Photos: W. K. Nash, used with permission.)

113

before its head breaks the surface. The heads of other animals behind it are clearly distinguished but the rest of the bodies are difficult to tell apart because the animals are swimming close to each other. Eyes are visible as dark spots on the head in the video. The closeness of neighbouring individual animals could readily give the impression of a particular animal having two heads, as in the sighting reported above by Dudoward.

The eyewitnesses noticed more details than are seen on the video…(bulgy eyes, spikes…). Nash sketched the swimming pod as it appeared to him. An interpretation of what a single animal might look like was also attempted; the flippers were not observed and are hypothetical. [37]

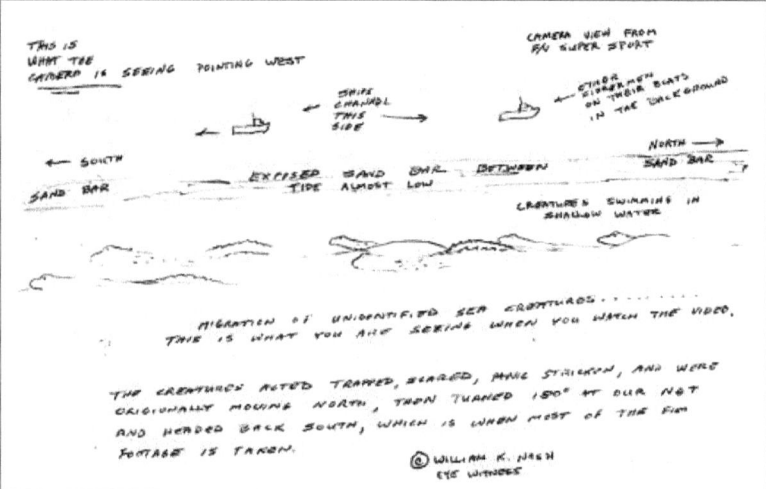

Nash's sketch of the swimming pod of cryptids, Nugashak Bay. 6:44:53 (Photo: W. K. Nash, used with permission.)

---

37. Images and sketches courtesy of Kelly Nash. Paul LeBlond and John Kirk independently and at different times, viewed both the raw as well as the stabilized versions of the video at Mr. Nash's invitation in Mount Vernon, WA, on May 17, 2009. The footage was subsequently sold to Original Productions, of Burbank, CA; a short segment was shown in a Discovery Channel episode of the Deadliest Catch starring the Hillstrand Brothers, Alaskan Monster Hunt and may be seen on the web at http://dsc.discovery.com/videos/alaskan-monster-hunt-sea-monster-witness.html

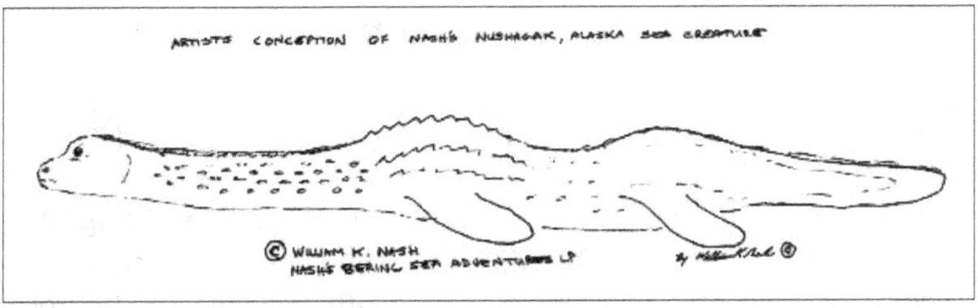
ARTISTS CONCEPTION OF NASH'S NUSHAGAK, ALASKA SEA CREATURE
© WILLIAM K. NASH
NASH'S BERING SEA ADVENTURES LP

Eye-witness appearance of one of the creatures seen and photographed by Kelly Nash and his sons. The flippers were not observed and are hypothetical. (Photo: W. K. Nash, used with permission.)

On the separate occasions on May 17, 2009 when Paul LeBlond and John Kirk viewed the Nash video, they both noticed one of the animals turning its head and directly facing the camera. The animal looked like a living, breathing version of the Naden Harbour carcass right down to the camel-like head and long neck. Its bulgy eyes could also be seen as it stared directly at the camera. These animals were certainly not narwhals as some viewers of the Nash footage have posited.

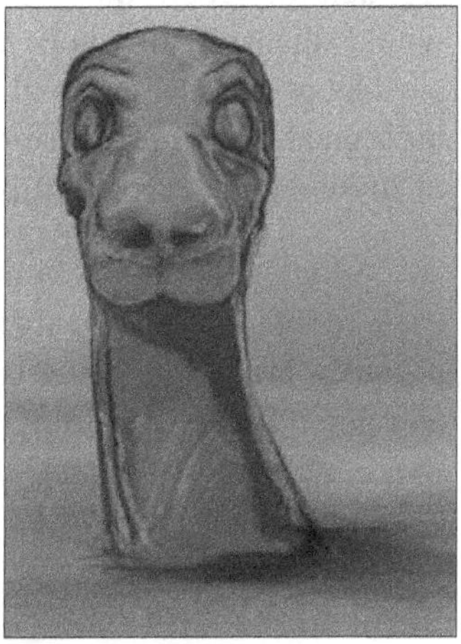

Drawing of the head and neck seen by Paul LeBlond and John Kirk. (Photo: J. Kirk/J. Walton).

Regrettably, that piece of footage was not from the camera whose footage Kelly Nash sold to Original Productions and aired on the Hillstrand program. It is feared that the footage was inadvertently recorded-over some years later and may be lost forever. We continue to enquire as to whether Kelly Nash may have made a copy on DVD, CD or on a laptop hard drive as this footage conclusively shows a group of Naden Harbour type animals alive off the coast of Alaska.

Besides a plethora of eyewitness reports, we thus have a handful of additional, if somewhat flimsy evidence—a mysterious carcass, a sonogram, an orphan photo and a video supported by witnesses—suggesting the presence of unknown animals in the coastal waters of the northeast Pacific Ocean and in some of British Columbia's lakes.

Chapter 9

How Many Northeast Pacific Marine Cryptids?

What is one to think of such a diverse menagerie of strange animals? Except for a couple of photographs—examinable records of what was seen by the camera—the evidence, in the form of verbal descriptions and sketches, is entirely based on eye-witness reports. In a court of law, under oath, such testimonies might suffice, but they do not achieve the level of reliability, accessibility and repeatability required of scientific evidence. There are some who would dismiss all such anecdotal evidence, an attitude which smacks of dogmatic denial, especially when there is no physical or biological reason for a priori rejection of the possibility of existence of marine creatures still unknown to science.

A logical approach in the face of such soft evidence is to assess each report on its own merits, as we have done, dismissing those possibly involving inanimate objects or familiar animals; keeping an open mind, withholding judgment or at least drawing only tentative conclusions. Scientific opinions on the relevance of anecdotal evidence in assessing the existence of large marine cryptids range widely. Speaking at a 2011 symposium of the Zoological Society of London,[1] Scottish biologist Charles Paxton opined that "reports from lay people have to be taken with a degree of skepticism," but also quipped that: "The plural of 'anecdote' can be 'data.'"[2] At the same event, University of Portsmouth paleontologist Darren Naish was of the view that: "The huge number of 'sea-monster' sightings now on record can't all be explained away as mistakes, sightings of known animals or hoaxes."[3] Just where individual scientists lean in their assessment of the value of anecdotal reports—somewhere

---

1. "Communicating Science: Cryptozoology: Science or Pseudoscience?" Zoological Society of London, 12 July 2011. Reports: http://blogs.scientificamerican.com/tetrapod-zoology/2011/07/19/ also http://www.theguardian.com/science/blog/2011/jul/15/
2. Paxton, C., 2011 as quoted in http://www.strangemag.com/recentadditions/understandseamonsters/
3. Naish, D., 2011, as quoted in http://dailymail.co.uk/sciencetech/article-2013773/

between "quite possible" and "most unlikely"—depends very much on their interests and inclinations. All such plausibility arguments can only be settled by firmer evidence: an actual sample, dead or alive.

So far, we have used the word Caddy for every unidentified animal sighted in the northeast Pacific Ocean. In this, we have followed the practice of newspaper editors who, faced with descriptions often contradictory or inconsistent, and keenly aware of the unreliability of eyewitness accounts, soon abandoned attempts at distinguishing and classifying such accounts. We adopt the attitude that Caddy may well exist and turn to the question: how many different animals might the term encompass?

Heuvelmans, whose systematic survey of marine cryptids was the stimulus for our own research, gathered 27 reports of sea-monsters in the coastal waters of the northeast Pacific, occurring between 1912 and 1962, and classified them into two types of animals. He grouped together all the "elongated sea-animals of large size characterized by a medium length neck, a mane, a horse's head and large eyes" under the label "merhorse," and offered a sketch where one would recognize many of the attributes described by Caddy eye-witnesses: a synthesis of Colossal Claude, the very equine creature described by fisherman N. Erickson, and the slightly less so encountered by Miller and Webb. Heuvelmans also proposed a slightly different category, the "Long-necked sea-monster," distinguished from the merhorse mainly by the length of its neck, as exemplified by the animal seen by Mrs. Stout off Dungeness Spit, or Mrs. Tildesley and Mr. Duncalfe a few miles away across Juan de Fuca Strait, or by the Hunts off the Oregon coast.[4]

LeBlond and Sibert[5] gathered 23 new sightings dating from 1905 to 1969. On the basis of differences in the size of the eyes and in body shape, they assigned the observations to three categories. One animal was characterized as having very large eyes, a horse-shaped head, a long neck (5–20 feet) and a body covered with short fur and showing three humps. Except for the absence of a mane, this animal was much like Heuvelmans' merhorse. The second type was similar to the first in general body type except for its much smaller

---

4. Heuvelmans, B. 1968
5. LeBlond and Sibert, 1973

eyes, the occasional presence of a long floppy mane and short giraffe-like horns on its head. The third animal was definitely more serpentine in form, swimming with loops of its body emerging above the surface of the water and a jagged fin running along its back. Its head was described as sheep-like, its whole appearance rather like the synthesis of early observations presented in the *Victoria Daily Times* in 1933.

Left: a "merhorse," and Right: a "longneck." Both images are of the description provided by B. Heuvelmans, 1968. (Photos: Authors' file)

Bousfield and LeBlond[6] recognized the possibility of there being more than a single type of animal seen by witnesses, but focused on describing a type represented by the Naden Harbour carcass and Hagelund's baby caddy, placing the emphasis on animals which they considered more solidly documented and giving the animal a formal scientific name, *Cadborosaurus willsi.*

In his analysis of global reports of sea-monsters, Champagne distinguished seven types, at least three of which pertain to Caddy observations. He characterizes the multi-humped type as having a dorsal crest and the ability to move in several undulations, as well as possessing a "cameloid" appearance; in his view, "identical to *Cadborosaurus willsi.*" Other types include two sizes of long-necked animals.[7]

Coleman and Huyghe distinguished two categories that included most sea serpent sightings: the 'classic sea serpent,' a composite

6. Bousfield and LeBlond, 1995
7. Champagne, B., 2001

of the many-humped, super otter and super eel types: a quadrupedal animal showing many humps when swimming; and the 'water-horse', a large pinniped similar to the long-necked and the mer-horse.[8]

British vertebrate paleontologist Darren Naish and coworkers[9] have also taken an interest in Cadborosaurus. They too have suggested the existence of a multiplicity of unknown cryptids grouped under the label Cadborosaurus.

A cursory survey of the eye-witness reports gathered here reveals some common types: the longneck "telephone pole" animal, often described as having a mane; the horse or camel faced animal; the more serpentine many humped animal, sometimes with a serrated back (much like the early synthesis published in the press in 1933). Other characteristics, such as hairiness, colour, horns, teeth, vary widely.

Following up on Paxton's aphorism about the plural of anecdote, we have treated the eyewitness reports as data and plotted the number of sightings in each decade from the 1880s. The large number of observations in the 1930s and 1990s are most likely due to the widely circulated publicity Caddy received in the press in the first period and to publication of LeBlond and Bousfield's 1995 book.

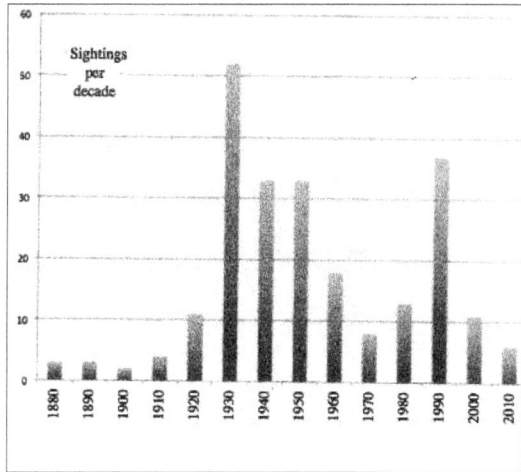

The distribution of sightings among the areas defined in Appendix 1 and in the accompanying chart tells us that Caddy has been seen just about everywhere in the northeast Pacific coastal areas, with particular frequency in inshore waters of the Salish Sea

---

8. Coleman, L. and Huyghe, P., 2003
9. Wooley et al., 2011; Naish, 2011

(Strait of Georgia and Puget Sound). As the number of encounters would be expected to depend on the product of the number of observers times the number of appearances, we cannot conclude that Caddy prefers inshore to offshore waters, but merely that it is more likely to be seen in the former.

Decade	Area 1	Area 2	Area 3	Area 4	Area 5	Total
1880				2	1	3
1890				1	2	3
1900					2	2
1910	1		2		1	4
1920	1	1		2	7	11
1930	18	11	2	11	9	51
1940	8	4	3	14	3	32
1950	15		5	9	4	33
1960	6	4		7	2	19
1970	2			3	2	7
1980	3	3		6	2	14
1990	12	4	8	8	5	37
2000		4	2	1	4	11
2010	2			5	1	8
Totals	**68**	**31**	**22**	**69**	**45**	**235**

Table 1: Caddy sightings in the northeast Pacific from 1880-2011, per decade. (Data from Appendix 1.)

Caddy sighting areas:
1. Juan de Fuca Strait
2. The Canadian Gulf Islands and US San Juans
3. Saanich Inlet
4. The Salish Sea: Strait of Georgia and Puget Sound;
5. Other areas, along the coast and inlets from California to Alaska. (Photo: Authors' file)

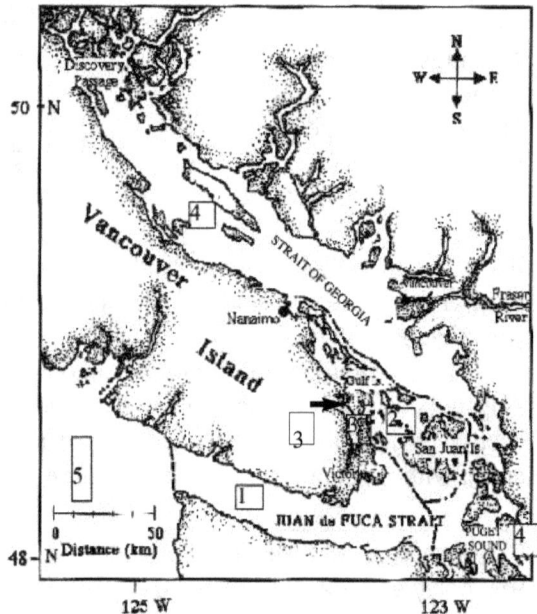

Large variations occur in the numbers of sightings within a specific area, for example in Saanich Inlet (Area 3), where Caddy is a frequent visitor in some years, but is also absent for long periods of time, not showing up at all for three decades—the 1960s, 70s and 80s. Such variations are not likely to be caused by a decrease in the number of observers (although it may reflect a diminished awareness on the part of potential witnesses) and may reflect changes in the animal's behaviour.

Some of the most frequently mentioned features include a long neck ("telephone pole"), a horse-like head (also camel or giraffe), humps or coils (like "truck tires"), a mane, and head appendages (ears or horns). A compilation of sightings where such features are explicitly mentioned shows that although there is a certain degree of overlap between "long-neck," "horse-headed," and "coil-humps" designations, they nevertheless form distinct groupings, suggesting a trio of different animals.

An astounding variety of resemblances are offered by eyewitnesses for the shape of the animal's head: reptile-head, python, giant snake and crocodile; dog-like, bloodhound, boxer, Airedale; eel-like, giant worm, frog; sheep, cat, giant sea-lion, etc.,... Whether some or any of these appearances, thirty of which are included in the "Other" category, are variants on the horse-like theme, may sometimes be inferred from a sketch provided by the witnesses (as in the Miller and Webb, 1959 encounter, where the animal's head could readily be described as horse-like, even though the witnesses do not explicitly suggest it). However, some of these other descriptions may reflect actual differences, different viewing conditions, or personal impressions.

Table 2:. Numbers of observations falling in three main categories (longneck, horse-headed, coils or humps) as explicitly mentioned in eye-witness reports.

Type	No Other Feature	With Mane	With Hair	Horns/ Ears	Serrated Back	Total
Longneck	32	4	3	3		42
Both	9	1	1		1	12
Horse Head	25	3	1	4	1	34
Both	8					8
Coils/Humps	46				1	47
Both Longneck	9					9
Other	83					83
Totals	212	8	5	7	3	235

Overlap between categories, for example when both a long neck and a horse-like head are mentioned, are listed in the intermediate rows labeled "both."

There are a handful of cases (not identifiable in the table) where all three main categories are mentioned. For example, the R. M. Elliott's 1917 sighting mentions an 8-foot neck, a giraffe-like head and 4–5 humps. Different head-shape interpretations might also lead to an overlap of the main categories: the animal sketched by Jim Maher (Aug. 1999) certainly has a long neck and shows a couple of humps with its "reptilian" head... which might have perhaps looked more horse-like from a different angle or to a different observer.

One may also imagine a long many-humped animal sometimes raising its head high above the water to appear as a long-necked many-humped creature. All this leads us to conclude that while there is evidence for three types of animals, there is some

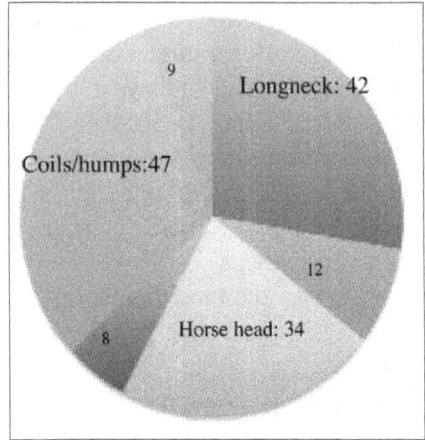

Repartition of 152 observations where witnesses have identified distinguishing features: a long neck, a horse head, and coils or humps, with some overlap indicated.

Area -> Type	1	2	3	4	5	Total
Longneck	11	2	1	8	20	42
Both	1	1	2	2	6	12
Horse-head	7	8	1	15	3	34
Both	3	1	1	3		8
Coils/Humps	19	5	4	14	5	47
Both Longneck	2	1	2	3	1	9
Total	43	18	11	45	35	152

Table 3: Animal type per area.

overlap between these types and the possibility that the same animal might be described as belonging to different types depending on its behaviour, viewing conditions or witness perceptions. We will continue to include all these types when speaking of Caddy, keeping an open mind as to just how many real different animals the term might include.

Long-neck types are more frequently seen in area 5, as seen in Table 3, whereas horse-headed and many-humped types are encountered mainly in the inshore waters of areas 1–4. All the animals seen in area 5 fall within LeBlond and Sibert's first category (long neck, horse head and humps). Again, however, the anecdotal nature of the information precludes any definite conclusion.

How long is Caddy? Witnesses often speak of "huge creatures," large and serpentine animals, "giant snake-like monsters"; some provide quantitative estimates of the animals' total length, sometimes with a degree of certainty, others within an estimated range. Statistics for reported lengths show a wide range of values: there are reports of lengths of up to 100 feet and beyond! However, the median of the distribution of quantitative length estimates is about 30–35 feet. Any further attempt at interpreting the lengths distribution must consider that there appear to be three distinct populations within this sample. The repartition of length categories among the three main types described is shown in Table 4. Surprisingly the median length reported is essentially the same for each category. Given that we are dealing with small samples of quite imprecise data, not much more can be said about this than that "Caddy is reported to be about 35 feet long, that being the median of reports ranging from 10–100 feet."

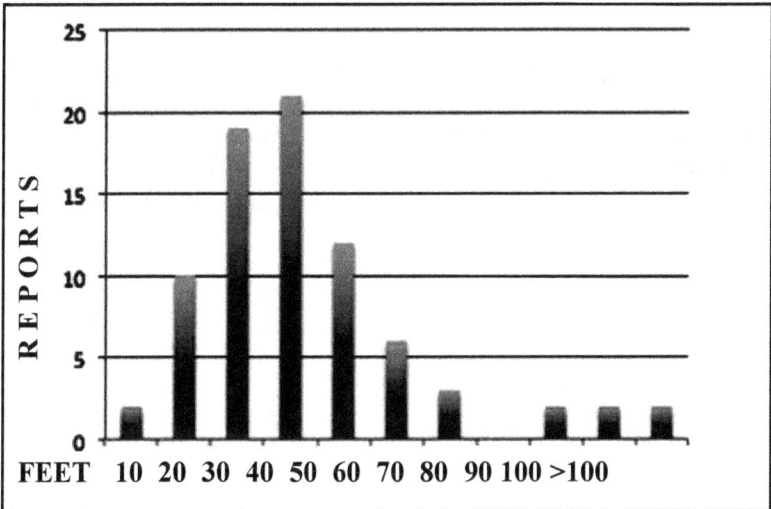

Reported lengths in feet.

Type-> Length - Feet	Long Neck	Horse Headed	Coils/ Humps	Other	All
0-10				2	2
10-20			3	7	10
20-30	3	4	6	6	19
30-40	3	5	6	7	21
40-50	3	5	2	2	12
50-60	1	1	3	1	6
60-70			1	2	3
70-80					
80-90	1	1			2
90-100			1	1	2
>100			1	1	2
Total Number	**11**	**16**	**22**	**30**	**79**
Median - Feet	**37**	**33**	**33**	**30**	**34**

Table 4: Total body length estimates for different body-type categories.

This cursory attempt at analyzing eye-witness observations should make the reader empathize with the frustration experienced by obsessively inquisitive scientists faced with incomplete, inaccurate and inconsistent data, and encourage everyone to support efforts at obtaining more reliable information.

Chapter 10

Caddy on Camera

Photographs are not subject to personal biases or preconceptions and can provide objective support to eyewitness reports. Many witnesses over the years have confessed to staring intensely at the animals they reported but reluctantly reaching for their cameras far too late or not at all. As a step towards more reliable evidence, we decided to take the rather impersonal approach of removing the human element from the equation and hopefully also the understandable mishaps.

Caddyscan was started in 1999, at Ed. Bousfield's suggestion, with the idea of setting up unmanned video cameras at locations where witnesses had recent sightings, as well as in areas where many sightings occurred in the past. We thought that having a continually running camera, focused on such locations was our best bet of getting clear video footage. Over the last decade we focused much of our search in Saanich inlet, a very deep and relatively narrow body of water lying alongside the Saanich Peninsula on Vancouver Island, and as we have seen, a hotspot for Caddy sightings over the last 50 years.

In the summer of 1999, Duff and Dorothy Waddell reported an unusual animal swimming by their residence in Deep Cove, Saanich Inlet, and we soon set up our first unmanned camera in their backyard, focusing on the area where they both had their sighting. Using a slow fast-forward, each video tape was carefully reviewed

Early CaddyScan view of unidentifed creature in Saanich Inlet. (Photo: BCSCC)

over the next few weeks, and although tedious and time consuming, the process proved successful when we observed a large animal that surfaced and swam slowly across the cove. While it looked unusual and had some similarities to the Waddells' sighting, the low quality of the video footage was not sufficient to make any conclusion and we quickly learned the importance of having high resolution equipment that would allow a better look at the targets.

After some upgrades and a few other camera locations, it was now time to make an important change from low quality video format to a high resolution Digital Video Recorder that can operate for long hours and deliver much higher quality images from motion-triggered events. The Gyyr DVMS 400 proved to be a formidable recording device, far ahead of its time in early 2000, with a maximum resolution of 750 x 576 pixels per frame and the capability of monitoring from distant locations while online.

CADDY SCAN
Locations

▶ **CaddyScan**
Members /contact
Media information

▶ **History/ Facts**
Sightings/Press

▶ **Research**
Reported Sightings
Stills/Photos
CaddyScan Media
Equipment

▶ **Monitored Locations**

▶ **Publications**

▶ **CaddyScan News**

▶ **Main Page**

Willis Point
Further down Saanich inlet and locale of many past sightings, CaddyScan monitoring location for 2 months in the Summer of 2000.

Deep Cove
Near the tip of Saanich inlet, set up by the local favorite "Deep Cove Chalet" restaurant, and local residence, CaddyScan monitoring locations in the summer months of 1999 & 2000.

Telegraph Bay
Set near Ten Mile Point near Victoria and location of numerous sightings, CaddyScan's digital monitoring site. 2002 - Present.

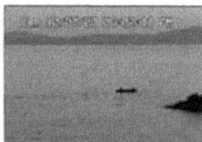

Saanich Inlet
Mid way Saanich inlet and locale of two recent sightings. CaddyScan monitoring location for 2 months in the Summer of 2004 - continuing 2005.

Now armed with proper surveillance gear, including closed-circuit TV cameras that would allow for zooming-in over large distances, we had at last found a reliable and practical method for searching for our camera-shy creatures.

Another witness, Bob Iverson, who contacted us with a sighting back in 1998, allowed us to set up a camera (now our longest-running) in his home overlooking Telegraph Bay—a post-card location off the Strait of Juan de Fuca, on the southern tip of Vancouver Island. The area is ideal, with kelp beds and a large diversity of marine life foraging inside the bay and just beyond.

So far we have recorded and viewed countless whales and sea lions proving the equipment is more than capable of doing the job, and only lacking the one element that no amount of technology or applied knowledge can ensure—a little luck.

High-resolution CaddyScan view from Telegraph Cove. The passing orca is clearly recognizable. (Photo: BCSCC)

Unidentified hump briefly seen off Telegraph Cove in February 2009 (amplified view in circle). (Photo: BCSCC)

Along with using camera recordings in our research, an Internet site called CaddyScan has been set up to provide sightings, history and other information on Cadborosaurus. It is at the following address: **<http://members.shaw.ca/caddyscan/main.html>**.

The site is maintained by the British Columbia Scientific Cryptozoology Club (BCSCC) and provides a reliable and confidential source for people to call-in or e-mail their sightings. Many of the more recent sightings have been communicated to us by way of the CaddyScan site, and we invite future lucky witnesses to contact us in this way.

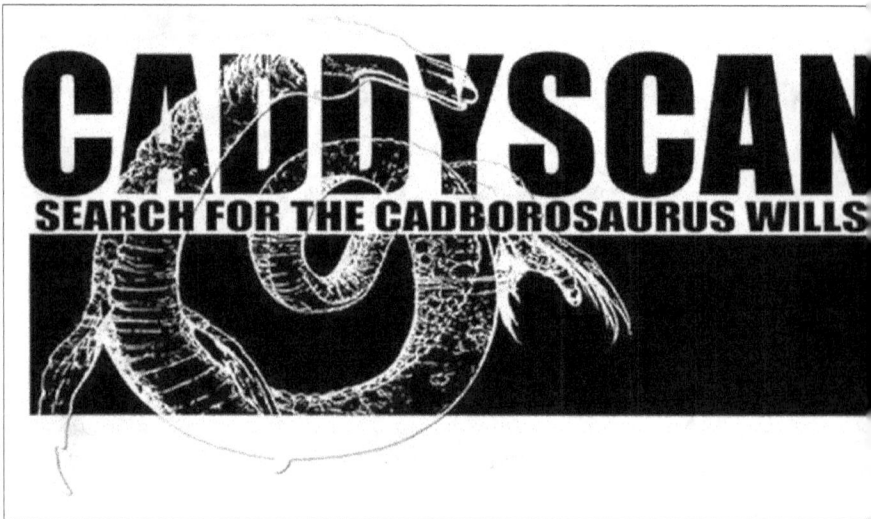

(Photo: BCSCC)

Chapter 11
What is it?

We now turn to the question which everyone asks: "What kind of animal might it be?" While everyone may contribute to the work of discovery, formal classification of new animals is best left to expert taxonomists. After reviewing some of the basic features on which such a classification might be attempted, we limit ourselves to summarizing the opinions offered by professional zoologists as to what Caddy might, or might not be.

We have already seen that the evidence available suggests that we are dealing with more than one type of animal, so that the features or behaviours observed may not apply to all types. Nevertheless, it appears that all types are air-breathers, as evidenced by their presence at the surface and the noises they make, thus eliminating fish and mollusks. Furthermore, most are described as undulating in a vertical plane, eliminating known reptiles, which wiggle in the horizontal plane. That they are fast swimmers and feeders on ducks, herring or salmon indicates that they are carnivorous predators. Other traits, such as their size, presence of hair, horns, colour and other apparently secondary features may contribute to their specific classification.

Dutch zoologist Antoon Cornelis Oudemans was the first to undertake a systematic study of sea-serpent reports. His first conclusion, based on about 60 reports available to him at the time (late 1800s), was that "the sea-serpent must be a mammal with four flippers, a long neck and a long pointed tail and that zoologically it must be half-way between the dolphins and pinnipeds." He boldly named it *Zeuglodon plesiosaurides,* the plesiosaur-like zeuglodon; the zeuglodon being a type of extinct primitive whale.[1] Some years later, after he became director of the Royal Zoological Garden in The Hague, he revised his views in the light of additional evidence, publishing a major volume in which he reviewed the evidence and reclassified the sea-serpent as a long-necked, long-tail giant seal, renamed *Megophias longicollis.*[2]

---

1. Heuvelmans, B., 1968, p. 312
2. Oudemans, A. C., 1892

Heuvelmans, in his encyclopedic review of the subject, re-examined Oudemans' data in the light of additional reports and opinions. Of the two types in which he grouped northeast Pacific sightings, he characterized the merhorse, which he named *Halshippus olai-magni,* as a "semi-abyssal mammal." While he did not explicitly state just what kind of animal the long-neck (dubbed *Megalotaria longicollis*) was, his analysis strongly suggests another mammal.[3]

Basing their conclusions mostly on the appearance of the Naden Harbour carcass and on the presumed relationship of Hagelund's "baby-caddy" to the large adult specimens, Bousfield and LeBlond suggested a reptilian nature. Their diagnosis was based on the likely cold-bloodedness inferred from the elongation of the body and on the disparity in size between the young and the adult.[4] Their proposal that Caddy be scientifically recognized as *Cadborosaurus willsi* (honouring Archie Wills), while following in the footsteps of Oudemans and Heuvelmans, was criticized as not satisfying the requirements of zoological nomenclature, which requires an actual specimen, not just a photograph.[5]

On the basis of the superficial similarity between a long-necked Caddy and long-necked plesiosaurs, it has been suggested that Caddy might be a "relic" plesiosaur, in analogy to the coelacanth, a survivor from a long presumed extinct creature. After debating the possible nature of the Naden carcass specimen, Bousfield and LeBlond suggested that Caddy was "…least unlike a plesiosaur," at least in appearance, if not in nature; not claiming that Caddy was a plesiosaur, merely that it looked like one. However, the subtlety of the double negative was misleading, and plesiosaur experts Bauer and Russell quickly responded to what they took to be a claim for the presence of a "living plesiosaur in the waters of British Columbia." Nevertheless, thanks to this misunderstanding, they presented extensive technical reasons why Caddy could not be "a living plesiosaur," a useful contribution towards a more appropriate zoological designation.[6]

---

3. Heuvelmans, ibid., p. 552-562
4. Bousfield and LeBlond, 1995
5. Bauer and Russell, 1993–96
6. Bauer and Russell, ibid.

It has been suggested that the merhorse type is merely a product of artistic imagination, inspired by the hippocamp, Neptune's horse, depicted in art since antiquity and still present in images and sculptures as an archetypal marine fantasy animal.[7] That there is a resemblance cannot be denied, as also the possibility that witnesses might have been influenced by their having seen, somewhere, a depiction of such a creature.

The sea-goddess Thetis (Achilles' mother) riding a hippocamp. (Photo: Public domain)

That not a single witness spoke of the hippocamp as a model for what they saw may however be taken as a measure of how little impact this artistic archetype had in their descriptions. In any case, the fact that observers of strange animals, in their attempt to describe the unfamiliar in terms of the more familiar, consciously compared what they saw to real animals, such as horses, camels or giraffes, or to extinct ones, such as plesiosaurs, or even unconsciously to mythical creatures such as the hippocamp, takes nothing away from their having actually observed an unfamiliar creature. The persistence of the hippocamp meme in modern consciousness may colour the interpretation of commentators but is never mentioned by observers and is entirely irrelevant to the existence of as yet uncaught animals.

To sum up, experts disagree on how many different animals may be grouped under the name Cadborosaurus as well as on their zoological nature. Many traits suggest a relation to marine mammals… oversized seal-like creatures, with a long neck, or a horse's head, or a long serpentine body. Clearly, what is required at this stage is not additional zoological speculation but better data!

7. Loxton and Prothero, 2013

Chapter 12

Conclusion

After reviewing over two-hundred reports, many from multiple witnesses familiar with marine life, we come to the obvious conclusion that these people have seen animals which they did not recognize. In most cases, the animals described are not only unfamiliar to the witnesses, but also unlike already known and recognized marine creatures. Caddy is certainly a natural, not a cultural phenomenon, although conjectures as to its zoological nature may be influenced by cultural factors.

Until specimens are available for scientific scrutiny, our knowledge of Caddy and of its freshwater cryptid cousins will continue to rely on random and unexpected encounters by mariners and shore dwellers. It is difficult to imagine that much progress will be made from an accumulation of such fleeting glances unless a better informed public—having read this book, for example—stands ready to take careful note of important details and, especially, to capture the animal in a photograph. While cell-phones and point-and-shoot cameras take adequate close-ups or scenery shots, what's needed is high resolution pictures, taken with a SLR camera and ideally with a telephoto lens. An armada of eyes on the water—alert to potential encounters, people equipped with modern cameras, and willing to report their observations to a central gathering point (like CaddyScan), may in time provide enough information to reach more definite conclusions. Photographs, especially when accompanied by eye-witness reports, will provide valuable records. What other means, technical or otherwise might yield more information?

We leave it to our readers and their friends to contribute to the discovery of Caddy and other cryptids. Perhaps you will be the lucky witness who snaps the high-quality picture that reveals Caddy's nature.

Bibliography

Bauer, A. M and A.P. Russell, 1993-96. "A living plesiosaur? A critical assessment of the description of *Cadborosaurus willsi.*" Cryptozoology, 12, 1-18.

Bentley, Mary and Ted, 1998. *Gabriola: Petroglyph Island.* Sono Nis Press, Victoria, BC.

Bindernagel, John A., 2010. *The Discovery of the Sasquatch: Reconciling Culture, History and Science in the Discovery Process.* Beachcomber Books, Courtenay, B.C.

Bousfield, E. L. and P. H. LeBlond, 1995. "An account of *Cadborosaurus willsi,* new genus, new species, a large aquatic reptilian form from the Pacific coast of North America." Amphipacifica, 1, Supplement 1.

Bousfield, E. L. and P. H. LeBlond, 2011. "Pipefish or pipe dream?" Journal of Scientific Exploration, 25, 779–780.

Champagne, B. A., 2001. "A preliminary evaluation of a study of the morphology, behavious, autoecology, and habitat of large, unidentified marine animals, based on recorded field observations." 93–112 in CRYPTO—Dracontology Special Number 1. C. Heinselman, Ed. Francestown, NH. (cheinselman@conknet.com).

Coleman, L. and P. Huyghe, 2004. *Field Guide to Lake Monsters, Sea Serpents and other Mystery Denizens of the Deep.* Tarcher–Penguin, N.Y.

Corley-Smith, P., 1989. *White Bears and Other Curiosities: The First Hundred Years of the Royal British Columbia Museum.* Royal B.C. Museum, Victoria, B.C.

Dalzell, K. E., 1981. *The Queen Charlotte Islands. Vol. 2, Places and Names.* Bill Ellis, Publisher, Queen Charlotte City.

Ellis, D. W. and L. Swan, 1981. *Teachings of the Tides.* Theytus Books Ltd. Nanaimo, B.C.

Fladmark, K. R., D. E. Nelson, T. A. Brown, J. S. Vogel and J. R. Southon, 1987. "AMS Dating of two Wooden Artifacts from the Northwest Coast." Canadian Journal of Archaeology, 11, 1-12.

Gaal, A., 1986. *Ogopogo: The Million Dollar Monster.* Hancock House, Surrey, B.C.

Hagelund, W., 1987. *Whalers No More.* Harbour
Publishing, Madeira Park, B.C.

Hart, J. L. 1973. *Pacific Fishes of Canada.* Fisheries
Research Board of Canada, Bulletin 180.

Heuvelmans, B., 1968. *In the Wake of the Sea-Serpents.*
Hill & Wang, New York.

Heuvelmans, B., 1982. "What is Cryptozoology?"
Cryptozoology, Vol. 1, p.1-12.

Heuvelmans, B., 1990. "The metamorphosis of unknown
animals into fabulous beasts and of fabulous beasts into
known animals." Cryptozoology, 9, 1–12.

Hill, Beth and Ray, 1974. *Indian Petroglyphs of the Pacific
Northwest.* Hancock House.

Howay, F. W., Editor, 1990. *Voyages of the Columbia to the
Northwest Coast, 1787–1790 and 1790–1793.* Oregon
Historical Society.

Kirk, J., 1998. *In The Domain of the Lake Monsters.* Key Porter
Books, Toronto.

LeBlond, P. H. and E. L. Bousfield, 1995. *Cadborosaurus, Survivor
from the Deep.* Horsdal & Schubart, Victoria.

LeBlond, P. H. and J. Sibert, 1973. "Observations of large unidentified marine animals in British Columbia and adjacent
waters." Manuscript Report 28, Institute of Oceanography,
University of B.C.

Loxton, D. and D. R. Prothero, 2013. *Abominable Science.*
Colombia University Press.

Mack, C., 1996. *Grizzlies and White Guys.* Harbour
Publishing, Madeira Park, B.C.

Mattison, D., 1964. "An 1897 Sea Serpent Sighting in the Queen
Charlotte Islands." *B.C. Historical News,* Vol. 17, No. 2, p.15.

Mora, Camilo, Derek P. Tittensor, Sina Adl, Alastair G. B. Simpson,
Boris Worm, 2011. "How many species are there on Earth
and in the Ocean?" PLoS Biology, 23 Aug. 2011.

Morton, Alex, and Billy Proctor, 2009. *Heart of the Raincoast: A
Life Story.* Touchwood Editions, Victoria, BC.

Naish, D., 2011. "A baby sea-serpent no more: reinterpreting
Hagelund's juvenile *Cadborosaurus.*" Scientific
American Blog, Sep. 26, 2011.

Oudemans, Antoon C., 1892. *The Great Sea-Serpent: An Historical
and Critical Treatise.* Luzac & Co., London.

Pomeroy, Lawrence R., Peter J. leB. Williams, Farooq Azaam and John E. Hobbie, 2007. "The Microbial Loop." *Oceanography,* 20, (2), 28–33.

Reimer, W., 1993. "Mary Clifton (Comox Elder)." *Gulf Islands Guardian,* Vol. 2, No. 4, Spring 1993.

Rendall, Belle (Evalina), 1981. *Healing Waters: History of Harrison Hot Springs and Port Douglas Area.* Harrison Lake Historical Society (1981)

Sanderson, I., 1970. "Alaska's Sea Monster." *Argosy,* July 1970, pp. 44-47.

Snelgrove, Paul, 2011. *Discoveries of the Census of the Marine Life.* Cambridge University Press.

Taylor, J., 1999. *River City: A History of Campbell River and the Discovery Islands.* Harbour Publishing, Madeira Park, B.C., p. 177.

Webb, R. L., 1988. *On the Northwest: Commercial Whaling in the Pacific Northwest, 1790-1967.* University of B.C. Press.

White, H., 1994. "The Cadborosaurus Meets Hubert Evans," *Raincoast Chronicles, Six/Ten, Collector's Edition II,* pp. 276–278. Harbour Publishing, Madeira Park, B.C.

Woodley, M. A., D. Naish, and C.A.McCormick, 2011. "A baby sea-serpent no more: reinterpreting Hagelund's juvenile *Cadborosaur." Journal of Scientific Exploration,* 25, pp. 495–512.

Appendix

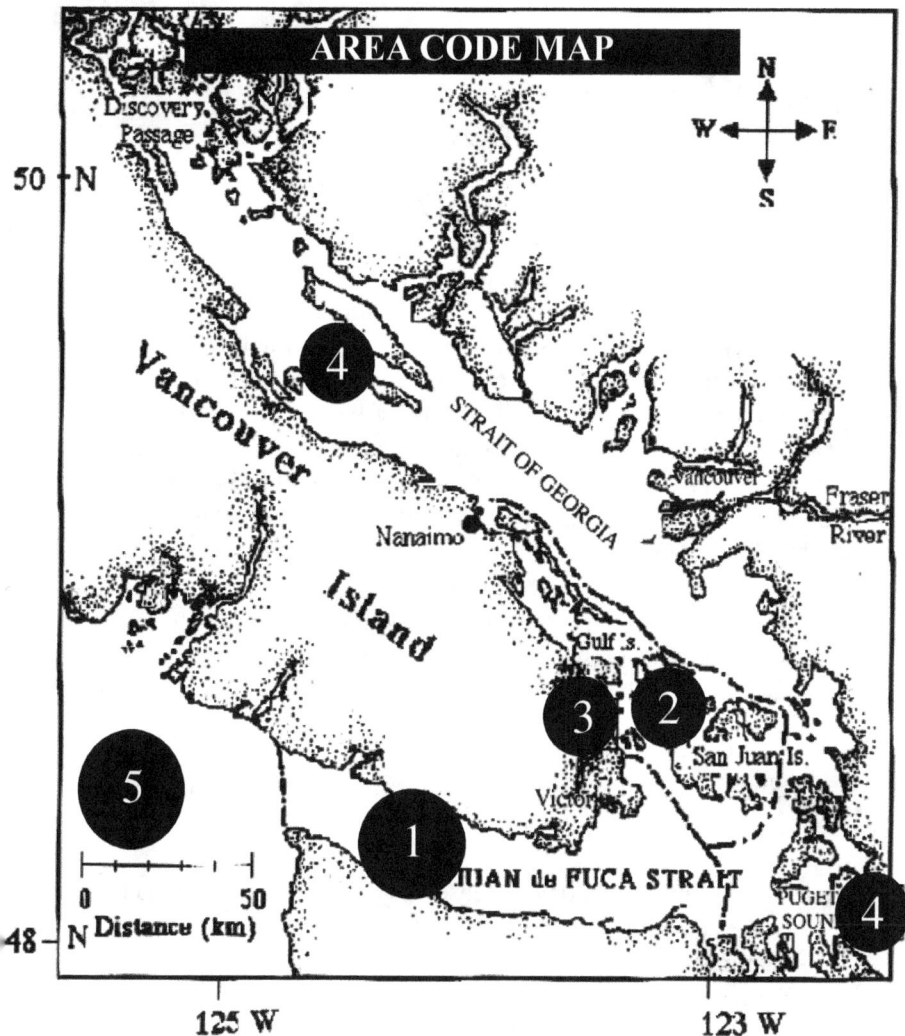

AREA CODE KEY

1. Juan de Fuca Strait, includes Victoria and nearby islands (e.g., Chatham, Trial and Discovery Island).
2. Gulf Islands: includes Canadian southern Gulf Islands and US San Juan Islands.
3. Saanich Inlet, BC.
4. Salish Sea: Strait of Georgia from Gulf Islands to Cape Mudge, as well as Puget Sound.
5. All other locations from California to Alaska.

Appendix
List of Sightings

This is our data-base of eyewitness reports. It includes only sightings which satisfy two criteria: 1) the object must be unambiguously alive, and 2) clearly not a known animal, because of its appearance or its dimensions. The list includes those sightings reported by Heuvelmans in the northeast Pacific (up to 1962); additional ones collected by LeBlond and Sibert (up to 1969); and all those listed by LeBlond and Bousfield (up to 1994). We have added older reports, lately discovered, as well as new ones which occurred after 1994. While we have searched extensively through press archives and widely broadcast our interest in this subject for many years, we cannot claim that this list is comprehensive. Indeed we know of additional reports which are not included here because they did not satisfy our criteria or because we could not trace back their source.

Sightings are listed in chronological order in the following format:

— Date (year, month, day or season as available); place, area code.
— Names of witnesses
— Features observed
— Source of information

Measurements are given mostly in English units (miles, yards, feet, inches) as used by witnesses. Area codes are attributed as shown on the map shown in Chapter 9 and on the preceding page.

Note: The chronological order of entries is as follows:

Year, month, and date known
Year and month only known (could be any date in the month)
Year and season only known, but placed before a month in the following season (could be any month in the season)
Year only known (could be any month in the year)
Decade only known (could be any year in the decade)

Oft-quoted sources are abbreviated and followed by a date. Example: TIM 5 Oct. 1933 (*Victoria Daily Times*). Similarly, other newspapers/sources are shown as follows:

Victoria Daily Colonist (COL)
Victoria Times-Colonist (VTC)
Vancouver Sun (SUN)
Vancouver Province (PROV)
Sidney Review (SID)
New York Herald Tribune (NYHT)

Earlier surveys:
Heuvelmans, 1968 (HEUV)
LeBlond and Sibert, 1973 (L&S)
Archie Wills' scrap-book (WILLS)

Letters or calls to contributors:
John Kirk (JK)
Jason Walton (JW)
Paul LeBlond (PHL)
Ed Bousfield (ELB)

Sightings
PRIOR TO 1899

1791 Oct. 16. Tofino Inlet, BC (5); John Hoskins' ship-mate. Huge animal with dog-like head and teeth; Seen on land. Known to natives as "Hieclick." J.C. Hoskins, quoted in Howay (1990).

1863 June. Off Point. Grey, BC (4); Thomas W. Graham and two First Nations men. "Mermaid" rose out of water—long yellowish brown hair... British Columbian, New Westminster, 27 June 1863.

1881 Summer. Nanaimo, BC (4); Frank Stannard. Had "folds." PROV, 24 Aug. 1940.

1884 Oct 2. Tacoma, Washington (4); John M. Barker. Animal 60 feet long, 4 feet thick, horns on its back. *Post Intelligencer,* Seattle, 10 Aug. 1951.

1888 Oct. Off Umpqua River, Oregon (5); Capt. Edgar Avery; barque *Estrella*. Animal 80 feet long, big as a barrel, head 10 feet above water, head flat, mane on neck. *New York Times*, 28 Oct. 1888

1895 Spring. Between Seattle and Juneau (5); L.H. Titus from steamer *Willapa*. "Reptile" head 10 feet above water, 18 inches across; much faster than boat; body 24 inches across. PROV, 21 July 1943.

1895 Oct 26. Bellingham Bay, Washington (4); seventeen people. Immense dark body, 150 feet long; 20–30 feet neck. *Times* magazine. Seattle 25 Oct. 1975.

1897 June 26. Queen Charlotte Islands, BC (5); Osmond Fergusson. Long neck, 25 feet long body. D. Mattison, *B.C Historical News*, 17, #2, 1964.

1900 TO 1919

1905 Summer. Johnstone Strait, BC (5); Philip Welch and friend. Long neck; knobs on head. L&S.

1909 Oct 2. Off Santa Barbara, California (5); Steamship *St. Croix*. Animal 60 feet long, head like eel, thick as a man. *San Francisco Examiner*, 2 Oct. 1909.

1910 Apr. 10. Saanich Inlet, BC (3); Two fishermen—quick look, hideous monster. TIM, 11 Apr. 1910.

1912 Aug. Johnstone Strait, BC (5); Hildegarde Forbes. Snake-like, 40 feet long; mane like sea-weed, 5–7 humps. HEUV, p. 445.

1917 July. Near Jordan River, BC (1); R.M. Elliott. Eight-foot neck, like giraffe; 4–5 humps—shot at it. TIM, 19 Oct. 1933.

1919 Aug. Mill Bay, Saanich Inlet, BC (3); Mary Lebel. Large green hump. Letter to PHL, 19 Dec. 1988.

1920 TO 1939

1922 May 22. Malcolm Island, BC (5); C.G. Cook. Long neck, large eyes, 25 feet long. L&S

1923 Year. Victoria, BC (1); W.B.Grant. Huge head, two eyes in front, whiskers; brown and shaggy. WILLS.

1926 March. Wright Sound, BC (5). Eighteen inches wide, 2 feet long head; 30 feet long neck. *Prince Rupert THIS WEEK*, 15 Sep. 1996.

1926 Aug. West of Queen Charlotte Islands (5): Capt. Obman, Fred Ellisas, B. Oban. Fifteen foot body out of water; immense head. *Columbian*, New Westminster, 26 Aug. 1926.

1926 Oct. Tahsis Canal, BC (5); Native fisherman. Huge creature with long neck. COL. 16 Apr. 1967

1926 Year. Cape Mudge, (4); J. Nord and Peter Anderson. Head like camel, 2.5 feet across, whiskers and mane; Fangs 6–8 inches long in mouth; fin on its back. TIM, 17 Oct 1933.

1927 Sep. Fulford Harbour, Saltspring Island, BC (2); Arthur E. Johnson and several others. Seasonal appearance; after schools of fish. TIM, 14 Oct. 1933.

1928 Aug. 24. Chatham Sound (5); A.J. Sprague (Fish Commissioner). Animal 300 feet long, greenish blue, 4 feet across—shot and hit it. *Empire*, Juneau, Alaska, 19 Feb. 1992.

1928 Late Fall. West of Vancouver Island, BC (5); James F. Murray. Head like a horse and lengthy neck. TIM, 4 Jan. 1954, HEUV, p.445

1928 Year. Harrison Lake, BC (4); two men. Animal 40–50 feet long, 8 inches in diameter. Belle Rendall, 1981.

1932 Aug. 10. Chatham Island, BC (1); F. Kemp and family. Large, serpentine, serrated back. TIM, 5 Oct 1933.

1932 Year. Roberts Creek (Sunshine Coast) BC (4); Hubert Evans, Dick Reeve, Bob Stephens. Horse's head, eye bumps, nostrils, ears/horns; long neck 12 inches through. H.White, *Raincoast Chronicles,* Six/Ten, pp. 276-278. Harbour Publishing, 1994.

1933 Early June. Gabriola Island, BC (4); W. McAllister. Spouted water from mouth. TIM, 19 Oct. 1933.

1933 Aug. 6. Burrard Inlet, Vancouver, BC (4); Edith M. Clark. Head like big seal and three humps; three times length of rowboat TIM, 20 Oct. 1933.

1933 Sep. 23. Cadboro Bay, BC (1); Dorothea Hooper and neighbor. Animal "like gable of house floating in water." TIM, 24 Oct. 1933.

1933 Oct 1. Chatham Island, BC (1); W.H. Langley and family. Animal 80 feet long, serrated back, camel-faced. TIM, 5 Oct. 1933. Interview with Mrs. Langley at http://www.cbc.ca/archives/categories/science-technology/the-unexplained/monsters-myths-and-mystery-great-canadian-legends/i-saw-caddy.html

1933 Oct. 12, Trial Island, BC (1); Mr. & Mrs. R.H. Bryden. Dirty green, serrated back like a fan; Spouting water with gushing sound TIM, 23 Oct. 1933

1933 Oct. 14. Chemainus, BC (2); Don Bellamy, George Neil, Harry Olson. Lying on top of water; left wake like speed boat. TIM, PROV, 17 Oct. 1933

1933 Oct. 14. Oak Bay, BC (1); C.F. Eagles. Head, neck, coil and tail totaled 60 feet; crocodile-like, spines on back. COL, 15 Oct. 1933.

1933 Oct. 21. Race Rocks, BC (1); Capt. W. N Prengel and First Officer J. Richardson, SS *Santa Lucia;* "upturned barge" moving rapidly, wake of foam. TIM, 21 Oct. 1933.

1933 Dec. 3. South Pender Island BC (2); Cyril Andrews, N. Georgeson, K. Georgeson and others. Swallowed duck in front of Andrews. Head like horse, no ears or nostrils; head three feet long, two feet wide. TIM, COL, SUN, 6 Dec. 1933. Live interview on http://www.youtube.com/watch?v=2FKO-nHAeHY.

1933 Dec. 4. Chatham Island, BC (1); Ellwood White. Head like horse, three humps, 40 feet long. SUN, 7 Dec. 1933.

1933 Dec. 21. Plumper Sound, BC (2); Cyril Andrews and Arthur Pender. Colour of ling cod; no serrated back. TIM, 9 Jan. 1934.

1934 Jan. 5. Fraser River (foot of Main Street), Vancouver, BC (4); Murray Jackson, Billy Alexander and three friends. Animal had 4-foot neck, head like a cow, two horns or ears. SUN, 8 Jan. 1934.

1934 Jan. 7. Trial Island, BC (1); C. and E. Marsh, and J.W. Chilton. Gobbled seagull, camel-like head. TIM, 9 Jan. 1934.

1934 Jan. 18. Bedwell Harbour, Pender Island, BC (2); Cyril Andrews, Arthur Pender and Eileen McKay. Animal 40 feer long, feeding on herring; gulls picking at it; dark stripe along back; not serrated; face flesh coloured, no whiskers. TIM, 23 Jan. 1934.

1934 Mar. 29. Victoria (off the breakwater), BC (1); I. McGavin and H. Sagar. Two animals (Caddy & Penda). TIM, 1 Apr. 1934, NYHT, 23 Apr. 1934.

1934 May 26. Off Cape Flattery, Washington (1): Capt. Landstrom and First Officer Connolly, SS *Dorothy Alexander.* Head as large as 40-gallon barrel. TIM, 27 May 1934.

1934 May–Month. Dundas Island, BC (5); W.R. Sampson and two sons. Animal 40 feet long, horse-like head high out of water at end of long neck; body like fuselage of flying boat; dogfish-like tail, with vertical fin 10 feet ahead of it. *Prince Rupert THIS WEEK,* 15 Sep. 1996.

1934 May–Month. Seymour Inlet, Nakwakto Rapids, BC (5); Sam Dumaresq, Tom Lynch and Ed Lynch. Long neck at 40° angle. Letter to PHL, 22 Nov. 1987.

1934 Sep. 11. Patricia Bay, Saanich Inlet, BC (3); May Williams.. Giant snake-like monsters battling black ducks; head like giant snake, 4–5 feet our of water, 4–5 coils. SID, 12 Sep. 1934.

1930s Early. Willows Beach, Victoria, BC (1); Betty Fraser. Undulating form, head higher than body. Letter to ELB, 12 Aug. 1993.

1935 May. Off Ucluelet, BC (5); Thomas Taylor. Animal 100 feet long, six feet across; head 2 times size of sea lion's. Port Alberni *West Coast Advocate*, 9 May 1935.

1936 Apr. 11. Cadboro Bay, BC (1); Arthur P. Dawe, Mrs. Dawe and Joe Smith. Camel's head, three distinct undulations; dived, came to surface to blow. PROV, 17 Apr. 1936.

1936 Apr. 12. Lummi Island, Washington (4); tugboat crew: Ole Kavande and Eddie Cadger. Animal 35–40 feet long, two feet through, dark grey; swimming at 10 knots. PROV, 18 Apr. 1936.

1936 Oct. Off Cape Cook, Vancouver Island, BC (5); Sig Trelvik, E. Clark and two others. Neck raised 6 feet above water; small head, large protruding eyes, light brown, covered with fur. *Port Alberni West Coast Advocate,* 15 Oct. 1936

1936 Year. Saturna Island, BC (2); E. J. Stephenson, wife and son. Three feet thick, yellow and bluish; sliding over the reef. *Advance,* Langley, BC, 22 Apr. 1960.

1937 Jan. 7. Near Crofton, BC (2); Capt. Cornfield and two crew members on tugboat *Solander.* Animal 35 feet long, looks like camel. *Cowichan Chronicles,* Vol 2. T.W. Paterson, Firgrove Publishing, Duncan, BC, p. 93.

1937 Jan. 11. Crofton, BC (2); J. Highsted and H. Dingee. Camel-like head, 6-foot neck, long grey hair, serrated back. *Cowichan Chronicles,* Vol 2, T.W. Paterson, Firgrove Publishing, Duncan, BC, pp. 93-94.

1937 Jan.–Month. Devil's Churn Oregon (5); William and Ila Hunt. Long neck, giraffe head, mane. L&S

1937 Apr. 30. Gabriola Island, BC (4); crew of Barge *Etta Mac.* Body 18 inches thick, mouth full of teeth, stripe brown and yellow, friendly eye. TIM, 30 Apr. 1937.

1937 May 2. Off Jordan River, BC (1); Mr. & Mrs. G. Meynell, Miss D. Meynell and Mrs. C. Belcher. Huge serpent, "glorified green garter snake." TIM, 4 May 1937.

1937 Summer. Sunset Beach, BC (4); Fred and George Lawrence. Camel-like head, small neck, barrel-size body, 50–60 feet long. HEUV p. 466.

1937 Early Oct. Queen Charlotte Islands (5); Fisheries Dept. Notice. Animal had 10 foot long neck with horse-like head. *Prince Rupert Daily News,* 18 Oct. 1937.

1937 Year. Campbell River, BC (4); W .W. Taylor. Five coils, 35 feet long, 1.0–2.5 feet across; very fast swimmer. Letter to ELB, 23 Aug. 1993.

1937 Year. Cadboro Bay (1); Mrs. M. K. Cole. Brownish, horse-like head, long neck. Letter to PHL, 14 Jan. 1985.

1938 Aug 11. West Vancouver, BC (4): Dorothy Burniston and George Wragg. Animal was 20–50 ft long; noisy; humps (seen by moonlight). SUN, 12 Aug. 1938.

1938 Summer. Taylor Beach, Metchosin BC (1); Fred Frudd. Camel- like head, humps (truck-tire diameter). Report to JW.

1938 Nov. 13. Oak Bay, BC (1); two local residents. Long head, jaws, fin on back. COL, 16 Nov. 1938.

1938 Dec. 6. Chemainus Bay, BC (2); crew of *Catala Chief* (coastal tug)—William Y. Higgs, George R. Macfarlane and John Shaw. One large animal (40 feet); one slightly smaller; vertical oscillations, snake-like head, round body. PROV, 8 Dec. 1938.

1939 Mar. 10. Victoria, BC (1); Mr. Jamieson. Animal 20–30 yards long, traveling at 35 knots, 5 humps. PROV, 10 Mar. 1939.

1939 Early Mar.. Chemainus, BC (2) Billy Shillito. Puffing/snorting; 30 feet long, five humps; head like horse; spray like speedboat. SUN, 17 Mar. 1939.

1939 Late Mar. Satellite Channel, BC (2); Bob Gaetz, Frank Marshall and Bill Smith. One large (40 feet); head bigger than, but like horse's; one smaller; hair on head and body, chestnut brown; no fins. PROV, 31 Mar. 1939.

1939 Apr. 25. D'Arcy Island, BC (2); Reginald Parris and Edgar Green. Colour of kelp, head like horse. Useless photos. TIM, 28 Apr. 1939.

1939 May 14. Nanaimo harbour, BC (4); Robert Morton, Thomas Hodgson and William Devlin. Light brown, horse-like head, large eyes, hissing sound, 20 feet long, 18 inches across. PROV, 15 May 1939.

1939 May 14. West Vancouver, BC (4); Jeannette Gannonx and mother. Three humps, as long as Dundarave Pier. SUN, 15 May 1939.

1939 July–Month. Oregon Coast, 90 miles SW of Columbia River, Oregon (5). Einar Lovvold and Harold Christensen. Neck and upper part 25 feet out of water; no mane, all grey. Letter to PHL, 26 Jan. 1988.

1939 July–Month. Off Destruction Island, Washington (5); P. Sowerby, R. Menzies and J. Layfield. Big head and eyes. L&S.

1939 Summer. Cadboro Bay/Telegraph Cove, BC (1); Mrs. C. E.Tildesley and Mr. Duncalfe. Long neck. L&S

1939 Year. Off Columbia River, Washington/Oregon (5); Chris Anderson and Jacob Lind. Camel head, 10 feet neck. John Grissim, *National Fisherman,* June 1991.

1930s Decade. Dungeness Spit, Washington (1); "Rusty" Beetle. Animal 40 feet long, serpentine body, head like camel/horse, with mane. HEUV p. 444.

1940 TO 1959

1940 Jan. 7. Victoria, BC (1); Cecil Burgess and Norm Ingram. Light brown, whiskers, long neck. SUN, 8 Jan. 1940.

1940 Early July. Patricia Bay, Saanich Inlet, BC (3); C. O. Biscaro and W. F. Hinde. Yellow head, fins all over the body. PROV, 12 July 1940, COL, 14 July, 1940.

1940 Mid Oct. Trial Island, BC (1); Walter Pratley. Bulky head and hump. PROV, 15 Oct. 1940.

1940 Mid Nov. Pender Island. BC (2); Roy Duesenbury. Head like horse, two blunt horns, 40 feet long, short neck, sound like rush of wind. PROV, 19 Nov. 1940.

1941 June 23. Nanaimo (4); T. Liston. Animal 20 feet long, 6–8 feet across; 2 foot fin on back; like a seal but much longer neck. PROV, 3 July 1941.

1942 Year. Long Beach, Washington (4); Frank E. Lawton. Picture taken. Animal 16 feet long, large flippers, brown hair. Letter to PHL, 19 Nov. 1987.

1943 Early Jan. Mill Bay, Saanich Inlet, BC (3); Mr. and Mrs. W. Gibson. Long thin neck, humped back, lunged at gulls. PROV, 14 Jan. 1943.

1943 April 15. Granthams Landing (Howe Sound), BC (4); S. Spencer and wife plus friend Mrs. Fisher. Head like python, 5–6 coils, 30–40 feet long, 1.5 feet across at thickest. PROV, 21 July 1943.

1943 Year. Trial Island, BC (1); Mina Peet and two sisters. Long snake-like body, thick as a big log, dark brown—"girls frozen in fear." E-mail to JW 15 Nov. 2000.

1944 Feb. 8. Keats Island, Howe Sound, BC (4); William F. Read. Large head, two humps. PROV, 11 Feb. 1944.

1944 Feb. 20. Witty's Lagoon, Victoria, BC (1); Eliz. Rhodo and husband. Animal 40–100 feet long, 3–4 coils; ate sea-birds. Call to ELB, Oct. 1992.

1944 Apr. 2. Bazan Bay (near Sidney) BC (1); Mrs. A.W. Collins and Mrs. Burt-Martin. Four humps, dark coloured. PROV, 4 Apr. 1944.

1944 July. Hornby Island, BC (4); W. Laurence Garvie. Head like sea-horse, nostrils, eyes, ears; snorting sounds, 35 feet long. Letter to PHL, 12 Dec. 1987.

1940s Mid–Decade. Burrard Inlet (Indian Arm), BC (4); R. E. Homewood and wife. Whinny-like sound; thick neck; horse's head; no eyes or mane seen. Letter to PHL, 29 Mar. 1988.

1940s Mid–Decade. Cape Lazo, Strait of Georgia, BC (4); Harold Hayes Jr., and Alex Somerville. Head like camel; two knobs like horns. *Comox District Free Press,* 17 Mar. 1949.

1945 Early Feb. False Creek, Vancouver, BC (4); W. J. Beattie and J. W. Wakeford. Airedale head; grabbed at duck; 10 feet long. PROV, 3 Feb. 1945.

1945 Dec. 19. Cordova Bay, Victoria, BC (1); Tom Plimley and wife plus 2 others. Camel coloured; long neck; broad hump, quite long. PROV, 20 Dec. 1945.

1946 Jan. Powell River, BC (4); Dona Morgan and Mrs. McAndrew. Horse head. Letter to PHL, 25 June 1988.

1946 June 24. Comox, BC (4); Mrs. S. H. Grist. Long neck, horse's head, red eyes; watching her dog. Letter to PHL, 9 Dec. 1969.

1946 July. Stuart Channel, BC (2); Ron Winkelman and parents. Horse-head, mane, ears, large round eyes. Letter to PHL, 9 Nov. 1989.

1946 Fall. Saltspring Island, BC (2); Dorothy Nielsen. Head like sheep; one loop seen; moved fast after school of fish. L&S.

1946 Year. Hecate Strait, BC (5); Capt. House, Fisheries Patrol. Like 30 feet long telephone pole. HEUV, p. 473

1947 Feb.–Month Off Siwash Rock, Vancouver, BC (4); Peter and Helen Pantages, and Chris Altman. Horse face, big eyes, 2–3 humps. Letter to PHL, 30 June 1971.

1947 Late April. Lyall Harbour, Saturna Island, BC (2); Mr. and Mrs. Fred Jackson. Head like camel or giraffe. SID, 20 Apr. 1947.

1947 May 16. Spanish Banks, Vancouver, BC (4); Frank McPhelan and Ron Kinlovh. Blunt head; pointed formation above the eyes Resembling a horn; big coil. *Seattle Post Intelligencer,* 20 May 1947.

1947 May 28. North Harwood Island, BC (4); Kaye Hanson. Big neck 3 feet out of water, humps; up-and-down motion. Report to JW.

1947 Sep. 26. Off Sechelt, BC (4); Marjory Tupper and Wilma Young. Head like horse but no ears, hump. PROV, 29 Sep. 1947.

1947 Late Sep. Mill Bay, Saanich Inlet, BC (3); Mr. and Mrs. George O. McKay. Immense forehead, mouse colored, no eyes or ears, 15 feet long. TIM, 22 Sep. 1947.

1947 Nov. Off Ucluelet, BC (5); George W. Saggers. Animal had 4-foot neck; jet black eyes; dark brown mane; wart-like rather than hairy. COL, 23 May 1965.

1948 Spring. Saxe Point, Victoria, BC (1); H.R. Johnston. "Plesiosaur"; small head, long neck, very large body, dark green; emerged; visible two minutes. Letter to ELB, 18 Aug. 1993.

1948 Late June. Useless Bay, Puget Sound, Washington (4); Rodney R. Hegelson. Anial was 50 feet long; back, serrated. Letter to PHL, 8 Aug. 1992.

1949 Apr. 12. Ucluelet Inlet, Vancouver Island, BC (5); Fisherman. Large, heavy snouted head, brownish yellow. COL, 13 Apr. 1949.

1949 Apr. 15. Cordova Bay, Victoria, BC (1); L. Tillapaugh and J. Corner. Like large eel, 25 feet long; noise like steam jet; bright orange brown. SUN, 18 Apr. 1949.

1940s Decade. Finlayson Island (5); Fred Dudoward, Bud Helme, Mr. Ivarson. Two headed monster, whistling noise, blowing spray. Letter to PHL, 29 Nov. 1969.

1950 Feb. 5. Victoria, BC (1); Judge James T. Brown, wife and daughter. Looked like monstrous snake. TIM 8 Feb, 1950. *Macleans* magazine, 15 June 1950.

1950 Feb. 7. Deep Cove, Saanich Inlet, BC (3); Mr. and Mrs. Stuart Wakefield. Moving along like giant snake. TIM, 9 Feb. 1950.

1950 Early Mar. Tofino, BC (5); Gwen Coleman and Bryan Tickle. Animal was 50 feet long, fins 4 feet high; cat-like head, long slender neck. COL, 8 Mar. 1950.

1950 Early April. Sidney, BC (1); Mrs. Dan Butler and, Mrs. H. Bradley. Small head like giraffe; brown, 40–50 feet long. SID, 19 Apr. 1950.

1950 Summer. Courtenay, BC (4); Hilda Keenan. Horse-like head, quite big; bump trailing behind. Report to JW.

1950 Nov. 17. Victoria, BC (1); Naval officer. Snake-like head, 18 inches across, large teeth; large flippers, flat tail, not serrated back; Large black eyes 2.5–3 inches across. TIM, 21 Nov. 1950.

1950 Dec. 1. Victoria, BC (1); Mr. and Mrs. A.B. Didsbury, Animal had 8-foot neck, 12 in across; brown, "sort-of" mane. COL, 2 Dec. 1950.

1950 Dec. 24. Oak Bay, Vancouver Island, BC (1); Doreen and Colin Andrews. Flat head, 4–5 foot of neck. Call to ELB, late 1992.
1950 Year. Departure Bay, Nanaimo, BC (4); Mrs. R. H. Leighton. Horse's head minus ears. L&S

1951 Mar. 30. Victoria, BC (1); Miss B. Morley and Mrs. D.W. Painton. Big square head, three shiny black humps. TIM, 31 Mar. 1951.

1951 Apr. Qualicum Bay, BC (4); Chet and Rose Charlton. "Three headed monster!" SUN, Apr. 3, 1951.

1951 July 21. Brentwood Bay, Saanich Inlet, Vancouver Island, BC (3); J. McIntyre. Brown, with dirty brown hair covering long neck; like camel with large eyes. COL, 22 Jul. 1951.

1952 Feb.–Month. Esperanza Inlet (Tahsis) BC (5); Fish camp manager and family. Eel-like neck, 16 feet long, whale-size body; flippers and flukes; mouth and teeth. COL, 16 Apr. 1967.

1952 Mar. 20. English Bay, Vancouver, BC (4); Reg Palmer and Bruce Mitchell. Animal was 20 feet long, big eyes, horse's head three feet long. SUN, 26 Mar. 1952.

1952 Apr. 14, Victoria, BC (1); Fraser Stanford. Body appeared smooth from one side, but with spikes when turned in other direction. TIM, 17 Apr. 1952.

1952 Aug.–Month. Northern Johnstone Strait, BC (5): Billy Proctor. Animal was 6 feet out of water, 3 feet wide. *Heart of the Raincoast,* p. 137, by A. Morton and B. Proctor,

1953 Feb. 12. Qualicum Beach, BC (4); R. D. Cockburn, C. P. Crawford, R. Loach, and 2 others. Dog-shaped head with 2 horns; neck like giraffe. TIM, 14 Feb. 1953.

1954 Jan.–Month McKenzie Bight, Saanich Inlet, Vancouver Island, BC (3); Ian M. Sherwin and Herbert Winship. Horse-like head; forward-looking bulgy eyes; Up-and-down motion; no fins visible. Letter to ELB, 24 Aug. 1993.

1954 Feb. 24, 25. Nanaimo, BC (4); W. Baldwin and many others. Horse's head; basking on water surface. HEUV, p. 507.

1954 Nov. 20. Victoria, BC (1); Jack Daily and Jack Salsbury. Head like frog; bulgy on top; fawn colour. TIM, 11 Jan. 1955.

1955 Jan. 2. Sooke, BC (1); Thomas and Marion Smith. Head like boxer dog, horns or horse-like ears; jet black and shiny; body 18 inches across and serpentine. TIM, 3 Jan. 1955, COL 4 Jan. 1955.

1955 Jan. 10. Victoria, BC (1); Mr. and Mrs. S. M Hobbs and J. W. Wyper. Light brown, nose about foot long. TIM, 11 Jan. 1955.

1956 Feb. 6. Deep Cove, Saanich Inlet, Vancouver Island, BC (3); Mr. and Mrs. C. F. Dalton and 5 others. Dived when plane flew overhead. SID, 8 Feb. 1956.

1956 Sep. 25, Oak Bay, Vancouver Island, BC (1); G. Kemperlink and S. von de Witz-Krebs. Animal was 30 feet long; revolving fins. TIM, 25 Sep. 1956.

1956 Year. Victoria, BC (1); E .F. Spence. Animal was 40 feet long, long neck, eyes. L&S.

1957 July 7. Strait of Georgia, BC (4); N. Erickson. Horse-like head L&S.

1957 Aug. Zeballos Arm, BC (5); Un-named man. Animal had 12 foot long neck. COL, 16 Apr. 1997.

1957 Sep. 13. Indian Arm, Burrard Inlet, BC (4); Job and Cecilia Smith. Indian name of animal Sayn-Usikh, meaing awful snake; no details. SUN, 18 Sep. 1957.

1958 Late Apr. Whidbey Island, Washington (4); John Oosterhoof and several others. Animal was 12 feet long, 1 foot thick. HEUV, p. 507.

1958 (or 59) July. Brentwood Bay, Saanich Inlet, Vancouver Island, BC (3); Mike Johnson. Single vertical loop like tire, 2 feet thick; Split tail tip. Call to ELB, Aug. 1993.

1958 Late Sep. Victoria, BC (1); M. McCord. Small horse's head; 3 humps; beard; barking. L&S.

1959 July. 19. Race Rocks. BC (1); Cameron family. Jagged dorsal crest; fast swimmer. SUN, 24 Jul. 1959.

1959 Late Nov. Discovery Island, BC, (1); David J. Miller and Alfred Webb. Long neck, hair like coconut fiber, big eyes. L&S.

1960 TO 1979

1960 Mar. 29. Smith Bay, near Crofton, BC (2); Everett Wilson and Scotty Henderson. Animal was 25 feet long, 4–5 humps, large black eyes. *Cowichan Leader,* 31 Mar 1960.

1960 May–Month. Taylor Beach, off Metchosin, Vancouver Island, BC (1); Frank Holm and family. Like a 30 foot brown log; moving fast. Letter to PHL, 23 Apr. 2009.

1961 Feb. 8. James Island, BC (2); John Walker. Animal was 20 feet long, dark brown; hump on back. SID, 8 Feb. 1961.

1961 Mid-Mar. Dungeness Spit, Washington (1); Mrs. Stout, her sister-in-law, and children. Long-neck, mane. L&S.

1961 Near Mar. 29. Off Sidney, Vancouver Island, BC (2); Mrs. A. R. Stacey. Head moving, seagull eaten (?). SID, 29 Mar. 1961.

1962 Feb. Campbell River BC (4); Mr. and Mrs. Alan Maclean. Animal was 18 feet long; snake-like head; hump on back; creamy yellow. HEUV, p. 507.

1962 Dec. 15. Lantzville, BC (4); Mr. and Mrs W. G. Clarke. Round, ball-like head. TIM, 18 Dec. 1962.

1962 Dec. 26. Lantzville, BC (4); Mrs. R. Guy and Mrs. K.B. Holland. Head like camel; big lips; large hump. TIM, 30 Dec. 1962.

1963 Feb. 12. Stuart Channel, BC (2); Mr. and Mrs. David Welham. Like giant eel, uniform grey colour. TIM, 15 Feb. 1963.

1963 Mar. 2. Off Gabriola Island, BC (4); Mr. and Mrs. R.A. Stewart. Huge head, gaping maw like hippo; no teeth or ears. WILLS.

1963 Near Mar. 7. Campbell River, BC (4); Mrs. Tom Conrod. Animal was 25 feet long, dark grey; had coils. TIM, 7 Mar. 1963.

1963 Mar. 21. Shelter Point, Texada Island, BC (4); Mrs. J. C. Durrant. Described as "like a big dragon," sandy colour, three coils at the back; hissing noise. *Campbell River Courier,* 27 Mar. 1963.

1963 Apr. 17. Victoria, BC (1); Un-named couple. Dark greenish; like eel; snorting heavily. TIM 18 Apr. 1963.

1968 Feb. 13. Juan de Fuca Strait, BC (1); J. Scott. Long neck; blew steam from mouth. L&S

1968 Nov. Ten Mile Point, Victoria, BC (1); Frank Holm and Sunday school class. Like big rotating truck tire 6 feet from boat. Letter to PHL, 23 Apr. 2009.

1969 Oct. 8. Cadboro Bay, Vancouver Island (1); Mrs. W.S. Foster and neighbours. Animal was 5 feet long, dark green, round lizard-like head—dubbed "Fidele" (Caddy juvenile?). TIM, 8 Oct. 1969.

1969 Fall. Ucluelet, BC (5) Wesley R. McCurdy. Animal was 32 feet long, dark brown, head like seal; long fin on back; spines 8 inches apart. Letter to Biology Dept., University of Victoria, 18 Feb. 1990.

1960s Decade. West Vancouver, BC (4); W. Kennedy. Serpentine head 1 foot across; grey brown, smooth haired—like seal. Letter to PHL, 9 Mar. 1988.

1960s Decade, many occasions. Tzartus Island, Alberni Inlet, BC (5); John Monrufet, crew and passengers of *Lady Rose.* Animal was 20 feet long—made great turmoil in water. COL, 2 Feb. 1961.

1970 Dec. 14. Foul Bay, Victoria, BC (1); Glenn Bertie. Head like a horse but longer; three fins behind head; body 18 inches around. PROV, 14 Dec. 1970.

1971 Summer. Westport, Washington (5); Rea E. Avery Jr. Animal had 6–8 foot neck, eyes, mouth, grey; appeared curious. Letter to PHL, Nov. 1971.

1972 Apr 2. Victoria, BC (1); Carl Hergt and Patricia Macdonald. Brownish, eyes like an alligator; lots of bumps. WILLS.

1977 Sep. 10, Bainbridge Island, Puget Sound, Washington (4); Ruth E. Kutz and family. Log that raised up, grey neck. Letter to PHL, 7 Feb. 1983.

1978 Aug–Month. West Coast Vancouver Island (5); Fred Pearson. Turtle-like with long neck. Letter to PHL, 26 Feb. 1988.

1979 Feb.–Month. Harrison Lake, BC (4); R. E. Probert. "Dragon chasing goose." Letter to ELB, Aug. 1992.

1979 Oct.–Month. Whidbey Island, Washington (4): Kathryn Schaff & husband. Blowing every 5 minutes; looked like a huge diver wearing a helmet. Letter to PHL, 26 July 1988.

1980 TO 1999

1981 Late Spring. Yellow Point, Vancouver Island, BC (4); Gordon Thomson and his wife. Animal was 30 feet long; 2 low humps, head and neck seen. Call to ELB, 24 July 1993.

1981 late June. Sooke, BC (1); Rudy and Wally Ewert. Greyish brown, no fins, fast swimmer. VTC, 29 June 1981.

1982 Aug.–Month. Secret Cove, Sechelt, BC (4); Louise Sanders. Like submarine periscope, 6 foot neck, small ears; colour of a wet seal. Call to PHL, 23 Oct. 1992.

1983 Early Spring, Pender Harbour, BC (4); G. Goff. Seen from airplane; large mass moving slowly; Took up whole width of entrance to Gunboat Bay. Call to PHL, 15 Dec. 1987.

1983 Nov 2. Seen 20 miles north of San Francisco, California (5); Marlene Martin, Steve Grant and Steve Bjork. Seen as 100 foot long big black hose; 5 feet in diameter; humps moving vertically in wave like motion. John Grissim, *National Fisherman,* June 1991.

1985 Jan. 3, Strait of Georgia, BC (4); C. Q. Cole. Turtle-like with long neck. Letter to PHL, 14 Jan. 1985.

1984 Jan.–Month Spanish Banks, Vancouver, BC (4); J. N. Thompson. Animal was 20 feet long; tan coloured head; giraffe like stubs; large floppy ears, eyes, mouth. Letter to PHL 22 July 1985.

1985 late Dec. Sidney, BC (2); Al Molberg. Head and neck visible. Call to ELB, 1992.

1986 June.–Month. Chatham Island, BC (1); Geoffrey Hewett. Animal was 20 feet long with humps. Letter to PHL, 11 Mar. 1991.

1986 July.–Month. Off Seward, Alaska (5); Eric Anderson. Head 6–7 feet above water; serpentine body trailing behind. Letter to ELB, 21 Apr. 1994.

1987 Mar. 1, Becher Bay, Juan de Fuca Strait, BC (1); Capt. G. Stephen Bain. Animal had 3 coils, sonar image. Letter to B.C. Museum and call to ELB.

1987 Mar. 28. Roberts Bay, Sidney, BC (2); Richard Smith and Ken Kilner. Animal was 60 feet long;, 2 large blue-gray coils. Letter to ELB, 1 Aug. 1992.

1987 June 1. Active Pass, BC (2); O. J. and Ruby Garner, Animal was 15–20 feet long; dorsal fin, bulgy eyes. Letter to PHL, 14 Mar. 1988.

1987 (Summer?). Cortez Island, BC (4); Allen Chikite. Giraffe-like head, long body, humps; colour of Arbutus tree trunk. Report to JW, 27 Jan. 2007.

1990 July-Aug. Cook Bay, Texada Island, BC (4); Frank Corbet. Animal was 20 feet long; large head 2 feet above water. Call to ELB, 1 Aug. 1992.

1990 Summer. John Island Passage, San Juan Islands, BC (4); Phyllis Harsh. Large head, 4–5 feet above water; two coils. Call to ELB, Aug. 1992.

1991 Mar. 30. Roberts Creek, Sechelt, BC (4); Sheila Bromley and relatives. Animal was 50 feet long; head, neck, 2 coils; large animal Call to ELB, 5 Aug. 1992.

1991 Late June. Ardmore Pt., Saanich Inlet, Vancouver Island (3); Terry Osland. Animal was 30 feet long; seen on beach—slithered quickly to sea; scrape mark and foul odor. VTC, 31 Jul. 1993.

1992 Jan.–Month. Gray's Harbor, Washington (5); Doris Sinclair. Animal had 5–6 foot neck; swim-dive motion. Letter to PHL, 20 Jun. 1993.*Pacific Northwest,* Seattle, Apr. 1993.

1992 May–Month. Cadboro Bay, Vancouver Island, BC (1); Prof. John Celona and daughter, Marjie. Head, neck, two low coils. VTC 20 Aug. 1992. Letter to ELB Aug. 1992.

1992 June 14. Cadboro Bay, Vancouver Island, BC (1); Michael Timney. Several vertical coils, 20–30 feet. Call to ELB, 1992.

1993 early Feb. Brentwood Bay, Saanich Inlet, Vancouver Island (3); Bevan Langton. Small head, horse-shaped, 3–4 feet out of water; moving fast, leaving wake. Call to ELB, Aug. 1993.

1993 May.–Month. Maple Bay, BC (2); Mrs. Patrick Cooney. Animal was 15–20 feet long, 2 humps. Call to ELB, 1993.

1993 July 14. Brentwood Bay, Saanich Inlet, Vancouver Island (3); James Wells and Don Berends. Two Caddys, 30 plus feet long; 2 low coils, gun-metal blue; Swimming faster than 40 mph. VYC 28 July 1993.

1993 July 26. Squally Reach, Saanich Inlet, Vancouver Island, BC (3) Harold Aune, wife and two friends—viewed with 20x scope. Animal was 30 feet long; splashing action—submerged after 15 minutes. Call to ELB, 3 Aug. 1993.

1993 (Summer?). Gabriola Island, BC (4) Scott McNeill and others on ferry. Animal was 35 feet long, multiple humps, head on long neck, rounded; smooth rhythmic swimming. E-mail to PHL 26 Oct 2001.

1993 Late Summer. Higgins Island, BC (4); Ray Lipovsky. Animal was 4 feet long, 4 inches wide; surfaced twice; offset knob on top (head?). E-mail to PHL 26 Feb. 1997.

1994 Mar. 19. Strait of Georgia, off Fraser River, BC (4); Capt. Thomas Ackman. Large Caddy-like creature, 40 yards away; head and part of neck seen for a few seconds. Call to ELB, Apr. 1994.

1994 May 5. Ten Mile Point, Victoria, BC (1); Ryan Green and Damien Grant. Blackish head, two truck-tire size humps. VTS, 6 May 1994.

1994 May 5. Cadboro Bay, Vancouver Island (1); Ron Minchin and his wife. Two low blackish humps. Call to ELB, May 1994.

1994 June 7. Clover Point, Victoria, BC (1); Mrs. Ruth Rodgers and her husband. Head and 6 foot long hump. Call to ELB, 1994.

1994 July–Month. Todd Inlet (arm of Saanich Inlet) Vancouver Island (3); Derek Colwell. Two huge animals playing in water; seen from Malahat Highway. Report to JW, 2000.

1994 July–Month. Roberts Bay, Sidney, BC (2); Dave Holt and 5 passengers in a boat. Large head and neck, 10 feet high; blackish green colour. Report to JW, 2002.

1994 Summer. Haro Strait, BC/Washington (4); Mike Grimshaw and other. Telephone pole diameter, 10 feet visible; no head or appendages seen. E-mail to JK, 2 Nov. 2001.

1994 Year. Cadboro Bay, Vancouver Island, BC (1); Michelle Boyer. Olive green, slimy, elongated body. <ufobc.org> 12/07/2006.

1995 Mid-July. Saanich Inlet, Vancouver Island, BC (3); Woman witness. Animal had a big head and two humps; smaller animal of the same nature swimming alongside. Call to ELB, 17 Aug. 1995. TC Aug. 20 1995.

1995 July–Month. Victoria, BC (1); Anita Newberry. Two huge humps, 6 feet from each other, air visible underneath; dark brown colour Report to JW 20 May 2000.

1995 Aug.–Month. Cordova Channel, Vancouver Island, BC (1); Jim Torrance, Tracy Maksymetz, Pam Bell and Terry Louis. Animal had 6 foot neck, red eye. Letter to PHL 8 Oct. 2008.

1995 Aug.–Month Howe Sound, BC (4); David Harris and others. Long neck; face like a large fist. TC 17 Oct. 1995.

1995 Sep. 2. Gil Island, Douglas Channel, BC (5); Roy Kristmanson and crew. Large dark eyes, head 3 feet long, 1 foot wide; Opening and closing jaws. Interviewed by PHL 8 Mar. 2007.

1996 Jan. 22. Esquimalt, BC (1); Ivor Cooke. Head like horse but stubbier; 5–10 metres (16–33 feet) long. TC 24 Jan. 1996.

1996, May 5. Ganges Harbour, Saltspring Island, BC (2): Les Bachmeier. Four large glistening coils, dark colour; vertical looping motion. Letter to PHL 23 May 1996.

1996 July 24. Mill Bay, Saanich Inlet, Vancouver Island, BC (3); Peter Gage and his wife. Coil eight inches thick, a foot out of water, blue-grey. VTC 27 Jul. 1996.

1997 July 2. Princess Louisa Inlet, BC (5); Tim and Laurice Mock, and son, Christopher. Animal like "large log"—splits into three parts and disappears. VTC 9 Aug. 1997.

1997 Nov.–Dec. Port Townsend, Washington (1)' Terry Graff. Three humps; rounded head, 1 foot diameter; 20–30 feet long; dark grey, smooth body. Report to JW, 2003.

1998 Year. Telegraph Cove, Vancouver Island, BC (1); Bob Iverson. Eight tire-like objects popping up; very fast swimmer. Caddy Scan camera site. Report to JW, 20 May 2000.

1999 June 8. Deep Cove, Saanich Inlet, Vancouver Island (3); Duff and Dorothy Waddell. Truck-tire thick, emerged three times; head observed looking away from witnesses. Report to JW, 1999.

1999 June/July. Cormorant Point, Victoria, BC (1); Tim England. Animal had 3–5 humps visible; not head. Report to JW, 2001.

1999 Aug.–Month. Mill Bay, Saanich Inlet, Vancouver Island, BC (3); Sharon Parsons and her son. Horse-like head, three humps. Report to JW, 2000.

1999 Aug.–Month Indian Island,, Tofino, BC (5); Jim Maher and friend. Protruding 3 feet above surface; reptilian head, 1 foot long; humps. Report to JW, 21 Feb. 2007.

1999 Summer. Knight Inlet, BC (5); Marie Hutchinson and Harold Aune. Blunt snout 2.5 feet high, 2 feet wide; very large nostrils, curved down mouth. Letter to PHL, 19 Jan. 2001.

2000 TO END OF 2013

2000 Year. Active Pass, BC (2); Ms. Lisa Lake. Long neck, humps. Letter to PHL 2 Aug. 2010.

2000 Year (?). Mukilteo, Washington (5); Cynthia Totten and family. Sea-serpent travelled slowly past. E-mail to JW, 01 May 2002.

2001 Jan. 18. Piers Island, BC (2); Carol Peaker and friends. Blackish animal, 15 feet long; snake-like head, one hump and tail. Call to JW, 23 Jan. 2001.

2001 May 21. Porlier Pass, BC (2); Alan Vittery and three others. Head like a giant worm's, 2–3 feet out of water; brownish—outline of mouth. E-mail to BC Scientific Cryptozoology Club, 23 May 2001.

2004 June. 8. Ardmore Point, Saanich Inlet, BC (3); Marjory Neal. Huge hump; went down "like a submarine." Report to JW, 2004.

2004 June. 19. Ardmore Point, Saanich Inlet, Vancouver Island (3); Marjory Neal and friend. Head, long neck, one huge hump. Report to JW, 2004.

2005 Oct. 29. Galiano Island, BC (2); Mark and Kelly Drake. Horse or snake-like head three feet out of the water; reddish hairy mane. Call to PHL, 2 Nov. 2005.

2007 June 30. Nushagak Bay, Alaska (5); Kelly Nash and crew. A pod of swimming animals; elongated, serrated backs, bulgy eyes; video shown to PHL and JK, 17 May, 2009.

2010 Aug. 16. Steveston, Fraser River, BC (4); John Kirk. Head sticking out of water 3 feet; 2 low humps; sank down vertically. E-mail to JW and PHL 16 Aug. 2010.

2010 Oct. 2. Pennock Island, Alaska (5); Two women with children. Camel-like head; 6–8 dorsal fins; exhaled from front of head and also dorsally. E-mail from Rob Alley to JK, 25 Nov. 2010.

2011 June. 20. Oak Bay, Vancouver Island, BC (1); Adele Kirwer and fiancé. Animal was 20 feet long, dark; swimming across waves; Looked like animals in 2007 Nushagak Bay, Alaska, video *(see this entry)*. E-mail to JK, 26 July 2011.

2011 July 25. Powell River, BC (4); Grace and Chelsea Murray. Up and down motion, semi-circle loops; dark tan colour; very fast swimmer; camel-like head. E-mail to JK, 2011.

2011 July 27. Richmond, Fraser River, BC (4); Sunny Fung and his wife. Animal had 5 foot long hump. E-mail to JK, 28 July 2011.

2011 Dec. 8. Deep Bay, Strait. of Georgia, BC (4); Coast Guard Auxiliary Unit 59. Large head, like oversized sea-lion; over 20 feet long; went down "perpendicular, without a splash." *Oceanside Star,* Parksville, BC, 15 Dec. 2011.

2013 Aug.–Month Cadboro Bay, Vancouver Island, BC (1); Aiden Girard. Large serpentine body—size of small car; head like seal or horse; 2 or more feet out of the water; looking around. Call to JW, 10 Dec. 2013.

2013 Dec. 14. Galiano Island, BC (4); Sylvie Beauregard. Black, glossy body; 3.5–4 feet out of water; 40–50 feet long, 20–25 inches across; head same size as neck; turning back and forth. Report to PHL, Dec. 27, 2013.

General Index

Note on inclusions: Items mentioned in footnotes are included only if they do not appear in the main text. Italicized entries refer to ship names or scientific names. Bold type page numbers refer to illustrations.

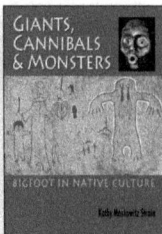